Praise for GOD ON FIRE

"This book is a masterful treatment of the nature and necessity of the manifest presence of God. Fred Hartley writes from the sweet authority of Biblical reality and authentic experience. A must read for all who long for revival and awakening in our day!"

- Bill Elliff, Senior Teaching Pastor, The Summit Church
North Little Rock, Arkansas

"A bold, winsome invitation to the emerging generation to expect, encounter and experience the reality of the manifest presence of Christ. Read it at your own peril! You could be ruined."

- T. V. Thomas, Director,
Centre for Evangelism and World Mission, Canada

"*God on Fire* stirs a new generation to believe for a move of God. I was personally stirred again. Thank you, Fred for calling us to all that God has for us."

- Jimmy Seibert, Senior Leader of Antioch Community Church and Antioch
Ministries International

"For those who have been searching for genuine spiritual renewal in their own lives and within the church, Fred Hartley's important new book offers fresh hope and encouragement; to settle for nothing less than the manifest presence of Christ."

- Garth Rosell, Professor of Church History, Gordon-Conwell Theological
Seminary

"In 1997, I used John's vision of Jesus in Revelation 1 to invite 1.5 million men to prostrate themselves before the reigning Christ on the Mall in D.C. and seek His manifest presence in our lives and for our nation. I'm thrilled that my friend, Fred Hartley, has taken those stunning verses and built an entire book about revival around them. *God on Fire* is powerful, hopeful, and inspiring. What a valuable resource for the coming Christ Awakening movement!"

- David Bryant, President, Proclaim Hope! Author, CHRIST IS ALL!

"Fred Hartley's poignant book *God on Fire* ranks with A.W. Tozer's *Pursuit of God* and the writings of Leonard Ravenhill in cutting through the miasma of "Christianese" and bringing the reader into confrontation with God's holiness, majesty, and consuming presence. Its straightforward challenge causes the reader to cry out for more of God, less of self, and to be God-filled. It is a serious *must read* for anyone who hungers for more of God's reality and power."

- Harold J. Sala, Author and Founder of Guidelines International
Laguna Hills, California

"One of the critical needs of Christianity in our day is to experience the filling and manifest presence of God—personally and corporately. In *God on Fire*, Rev. Fred Hartley shows how God has taken the initiative to invite us to experience His presence daily. Using ample illustrations from Scripture and Church history, Hartley walks readers through the Apostle John's Patmos experience of the manifest presence of Christ and closes each chapter with important takeaways and practical application. This book belongs in the library of every follower of Jesus and is a valuable encouragement and resource for the Spirit-filled life."

- Gary M. Benedict, President of the U.S. Christian and Missionary Alliance
Colorado Springs, Colorado

"I have always loved reading and studying about revivals! This book has become one of my favorites! This heart-stirring and refreshing work by Fred Hartley captures not only the essence of revival, but a much needed theology of revival. My heart was stirred with desire as I read this book and I'm sure your heart will also be challenged with a similar desire to experience afresh the 'manifest presence' of God. This book is a must read. Its clear focus on the centrality of Christ, the easy reading style, the illustrations from history, and the simple chapter takeaways all make this book a real winner and a great gift to others."

- Dr. Dann Spader, President, Global Youth Initiative and Founder, Sonlife Ministries
Equipping the next generation to live out both the passion and priorities of Jesus

"Fred Hartley writes about fire from a heart that's always burning—burning to know Jesus more and to make Him known everywhere. He lives to see hearts on fire and joined together to create churches on fire. This, in turn, will set cities and nations on fire for God. Read him; then get a match."

- Mark DeMoss, Founder, The DeMoss Group
Atlanta, Georgia

"It is indeed a great privilege for me to tell others about Fred Hartley, the author of *God on Fire*. His life impacts thousands of lives for Christ in a dynamic way. As a result of Fred's prayer life *Prayer on Fire*, his last book, was written to let readers know how to encounter God's manifest presence. This led him to write *God on Fire, Encountering the Manifest Presence of Christ* which is probably one of the most incredible books ever written and a must-read for the church of Christ. Expect a life-changing experience! It is my desire for you, the reader, to experience for yourself the awesome blessings intended for you."

- Burtram Sorensen, Former Partner, Goldman Sachs Investment Firm
New York City, NY

"With his latest and perhaps most important book, Fred Hartley offers readers tremendous insight into experiencing the manifest presence of God. He shows through Scripture and in history how God ignites His manifest presence in the lives of His own. How does God reveal Himself? How can we know it is really Him? How can we prepare our hearts and lives for such a revelation? And after the revelation comes, how do we respond? These are just some of the questions Hartley asks—and answers. You may never read a more life-changing book. You may never find a clearer map to personal revival; to living in the fiery presence of our Lord. The church needs this book."

- Michael G. Scales, Ed.D., President, Nyack College & Alliance Theological Seminary

"The world is in desperate need of a new generation of revivalists after God's Heart and His Manifest Presence. My dear brother Fred Hartley provides a perfect incubator for the seeds of a new generation in his book, *God on Fire, Encountering the Manifest Presence of Christ*. Nothing will transform the Church and our world like the manifest presence of *God on Fire*! This book inspires passion in my soul to pursue that presence at all costs. 'Come Holy Spirit!' Nothing like this has been written until now."

- Ron Walborn, Dean of Alliance Theological Seminary and the College of Bible and Ministry, Nyack College, Nyack, New York

"I always love Pastor Fred Hartley's books. They create a new zeal for Jesus in me and I enthusiastically recommend *God on Fire: Encountering the Manifest Presence of Christ*. In the church today there is a problem. Most Christians are looking for a manifestation and not the manifest presence of God. When the manifest presence of God is experienced, no one leaves such an encounter wondering if God was there. You are forever changed. And I love how Pastor Fred so beautifully weaves together the stories of men and women in history that God used to bring revival fire into their culture. This is our time; our day to be history makers. So this amazing God-anointed book begs us to cry out, 'Consume us by your fire, oh Lord!' Don't overlook this opportunity to be changed. You can thank me later."

- Dr. Alice Smith, U.S. Prayer Center Houston, Texas

"If you can't wait a moment more for a fresh encounter with God, then *God on Fire* is for you. I must warn you, *God on Fire* isn't a quiet message nor is it tame. It is a clarion call with all the vibrancy of a fireworks show. I can't wait to put this in the hands of every pastor I know. You can be sure of this: the voltage of your friendship with God is about to rise."

- Jonathan Gulley, Lead Pastor of Antioch Community Church Wheaton, Illinois

"In the past season of my life, no writer has impacted my personal Christian walk and ministry like Fred Hartley. His passion for the manifest presence of God and encountering Christ through intentional prayer has greatly inspired me to seek God like never before. In *God on Fire*, Fred once again brought me face to face with the call not just to seek the One who delights to make His presence known, but to lead His church in this generation to do the same."

- Chip Henderson, Senior Pastor, Pinelake Church,
Brandon, Mississippi

"If the ambition of this book is realized, the results could be daunting. Imagine students seeking an awareness of God's presence with no appetite for cold, life-less religious expressions. May it be in this generation! While I would express some aspects of God's manifest presence differently, I thank God for the life message of Fred Hartley, especially his passion for students. He has been encouraging me with his writing for 30 years!"

- Steven Smith, Dean of the College of Southwestern and Professor of
Communication
Southwestern Baptist Theological Seminary
Ft. Worth, Texas

"Don't read this book! Not until you have pulled the straps tight because you are about to leave the station on a spiritually-disruptive, conscience-provoking deep-dive into the manifest presence of God! A job transfer took me away from the weekly ministry of Fred Hartley several years ago but it only took a few pages to realize *God on Fire* is classic 'Pastor Fred'—pushing, poking and prodding the status quo as I've seen God do through him many times before. Yes, the gentle work of the Holy Spirit is evident throughout, but be prepared. *God on Fire* is not comfortable. It will shine a light in dark corners, stalk off-limit hallways and pry open tightly locked doors. Indeed, *God on Fire* should come with a warning label: 'Enter with Caution. You will not leave the same as you came in!' Hartley says the book will 'ruin you.' So let it. You'll like what God will do with what's left."

- John Towriss, Principal, Envoy Strategy Group
Washington, DC

"In *God on Fire* Fred Hartley takes us on a historical journey of how God's all-encompassing fire possessed many of the early saints as they entreated to God in prayer. I learned so much! And I was challenged to go deeper in my own prayer life so that I too might experience the fire of God's presence in my own life. This is a book for every serious follower of Jesus Christ. When we experience God's manifest presence it moves us out of complacency into a heart on fire for God. Read this book! But beware; you may just catch on fire!"

- Os Hillman, Author, *TGIF Today God Is First* and *Change Agent*

God on Fire is awe-inspiring, challenging, convicting, fire-stoking, encouraging, purifying, empowering, eye-opening, and so much more. For nearly twenty years,

I have known Fred Hartley to be a man in pursuit of the Lord with his face set like flint to know Him and make Him known. This book is not born out of theory or theological platitudes, but out of a journey of allowing God on fire to ignite and fuel revival fires in a human vessel, no matter the cost. *God on Fire* reveals the reality of God as both the source and the object of all who would live in pursuit of a full-blown, fire-fueled, Holy Spirit revival in our day. It is my honor to endorse and encourage others to read this book, but more so to join the growing company of folks who are both being pursued and pursuing *God on Fire!*"

- Jacquie Tyre, Kairos Transformation Ministries- City Gate
Atlanta, Georgia

"In *God on Fire*, Fred Hartley summarizes and describes what theologians and biblical scholars have tried to do in many volumes, specifically speaking about the nearness of God, His absolute desire to make things new, and His love for His creation, the human beings whom He created to fellowship with Him and live in His warm presence. Humans like [me] and you who are made to walk with Him, unlike all other creatures. Humans created in his image to be able to communicate with Him, and live for Him.

Fred Hartley is pushing us to maximize our limits and to reach God's limits in order to be able to immerse in His fiery presence, which we can only do through the cleansing of the holy blood of Jesus and through being filled with His Spirit and Word. The people of God nowadays are in utmost need for God's manifest presence, a presence that makes an impact like no other. That's why, we ought— rather we should—seek, desire, and dedicate ourselves to God's manifest presence.

I endorse this book whole heartedly for any Christian who is thirsty for more; who is hungry for much a bigger fill than anything the world can give. I promise you, upon reading and absorbing it, you will be a totally changed person."

- Rev. Jack Y. Sara, President, Bethlehem Bible College
Bethlehem

GOD
on
FIRE

Encountering the Manifest Presence of Christ

Fred A. Hartley, III

PUBLICATIONS

Fort Washington, PA 19034

God on Fire:
Encountering the Manifest Presence of Christ

Published by CLC Publications, U.S.A.
P.O. Box 1449, Fort Washington, PA 19034

Printed in the United States of America
First Printing 2012

ISBN-10 (trade paper): 1-61958-012-8
ISBN-13 (trade paper): 978-1-61958-012-1
ISBN-13 (e-book): 978-1-61958-066-4

Dedication

To my two college-student sons,
Stephen and Andrew[1],
and to everyone in your generation who longs to encounter
the sin-crushing,
satan-evicting,
Christ-exalting,
life-transforming,
nation-discipling,
raging inferno of God's manifest presence.
Have at it!
I dedicate this book to you
with the promise that God is on fire.

Table of Contents

Foreword

THERE are always two incredibly glorious things that happen in times of true revival: the manifest presence of Christ saturates the church and the word of God flows forth like a mighty tidal wave of divine blessing upon a dry and thirsty world. The manifest presence of Christ in the church immediately reveals the filth of sin and the vast array of encumbrances and weights which have hindered effective spiritual growth and ministry both in the church and in the lives of individual believers. This is accompanied by a mighty outpouring of the dual precious gifts of repentance and faith which results in a wonderfully transformed and revitalized body of individual believers and churches. Our radiant countenances and glowing testimonies profoundly impact all who know us. Combine this with the Word of God itself pouring forth from the pulpits and the lips of the revived, and the result is the true conversion of multitudes; an awakening in the world.

Fred Hartley, in this much needed book, brings to the forefront this vital biblical teaching on the manifest presence of Christ in the church.

In the last of six warning passages in Hebrews 12:25-29, the author declares: "For our God is a consuming fire." From verses 18 to 24, the author contrasts the experience of Israel coming to Mount Sinai, where God gave them the law, with the Christian's experience of coming to Christ. "For you have come to Mount Zion and to the city of the living God, the heavenly Jerusalem ..." (verses 22-24). He then warns in verse 25, "See that you do not refuse Him who speaks. For if they did not escape who refused Him who spoke on earth, much more shall we not escape if we turn away from Him who speaks from heaven." Throughout Hebrews the solid Biblical principle of "to whom much has been given, much will be required" is illustrated.

There can be no question that New Testament Christians received vastly more from Christ than Old Testament believers, and are thus much more obliged to respond with far greater love and devotion. In verses 26-27, we are told, "[He] whose voice then shook the earth; but now He has promised, saying, 'Yet once more I shake not only the earth, but also heaven.' Now this, 'yet once more,' indicates the removal of those things that are being shaken, as of things that are made, that the things which cannot be shaken may remain."

Every wise reader must ask, *what will be shaken out of my life at this great shaking?* And in the light of verse 28, "Therefore, since we are receiving a kingdom which cannot be shaken, let us have grace, by which we may serve God acceptably with reverence and godly fear. For our God is a consuming fire (verses 28-29).

In Luke 3:16, John the Baptist draws two potent contrasts. The first contrast is between his person and the person of Christ. This leads him to declare, "He who is mightier than I is coming, and I am not fit to untie the thong of His sandals." The second contrast is between his baptism and the baptism of Christ. "As for me, I baptize you with water; but...He will baptize you in the Holy Spirit and power." The baptism of the Holy Spirit is clearly a baptism of power. But of what does the baptism of fire speak?

We noted in Hebrews, "Our God is a consuming fire." A consuming fire can be both negative and positive. Negative in that it destroys. Positive in that it purifies. Hebrews notes that everything shaken out will be consumed in fire. Luke 3:9 declares that "the axe is already laid at the root of the trees; every tree therefore that does not bear good fruit is cut down and thrown into the fire." In Luke 3:17 we also read, "And His winnowing fork is in His hand to clean out His threshing floor, and to gather the wheat into His barn; but He will burn up the chaff with unquenchable fire." In both these verses, the fire is destructive. But the baptism of fire in Jesus Christ is positive. It is the refiner's fire that results in two great blessings for all its recipients: passion and purity. Exactly what today's church desperately needs!

As you read this book, may the manifest presence of Christ envelop you. May His precious presence work as the refiner's fire, burning out of your life everything that hinders the glory of God from adorning you. May His manifest presence serve as an igniter, setting all your passions for Christ and His kingdom on fire and kindling your very soul with the fire of God for the salvation of a lost and dying world.

May this book you hold in your hands help to change your life and our world forever!

Richard Owen Roberts

Introduction

An Open Letter to College Students

AS college and university students, I love your passion. I love your pursuit of reality and your zeal for the journey. You inspire me! I admire your refusal to settle for hollow religious traditions that are superficial or meaningless. Many of you are sick and tired of irrelevant church politics and phony religious leaders who lack integrity. Some of you have dared to say, "Jesus? Yes! The church? No!" And to some extent I don't blame you. In many ways my generation has poorly modeled what Christianity is all about.

Surely there must be more to church than keeping the religious machinery moving, you say. You don't want to be identified with plastic people who say predictable prayers and listen to leftover sermons. Quite frankly, I don't either.

There is an answer to both the lukewarm church and lukewarm hearts. The answer is *God on fire*. Untamed. Unpredictable. Revolutionary. Righteous. Reviving.

God on fire is the manifest presence of Christ. We don't need to talk about it. We need an encounter. It is the one true God who loves to roll up His sleeves, flex His biceps and conspicuously show Himself to us right down the middle of our lives. Fire is the antithesis of anything lukewarm.

Encountering *God on fire* is the answer not only for our lukewarm hearts but for our lukewarm congregations.

Allow me to clarify something. There is a significant difference between human passion and *God on fire*. Passion is our response; fire is God's initiative. When the self-revealing God chooses to make His presence known, it is His work, not ours.

People who hear me preach often tell me, "You're sure on fire!" I appreciate the compliment, but I do not want people to confuse emotional intensity with the fire of God. Revival in its truest sense is the study of what happens when God's people reencounter His manifest presence. The problem with the study of revival is that people shift the focus from the God who manifests Himself to the response of God's people. Even worse, it carries with it all sorts of baggage—emotionalism, fanaticism and excess. At best, it puts the emphasis on the effect rather than the cause. The body of Christ needs to put the focus where it belongs: on God, not on us. For the next one hundred pages, I will do my absolute best to put the focus on what God does to encounter *us*.

My wife and I recently visited with Richard Owen Roberts, one of the most trusted scholars in the history of revival. Roberts owns one of the most extensive private revival libraries in the world. We sat in his study, surrounded by tens of thousands of revival books. Roberts talked affectionately about the manifest presence of God. His eyes moistened as he freely talked with me as a kindred spirit about the passion of his life—the presence of God. As I told him about my goal to write a biblical theology of revival and the defense of the manifest presence of God, I was startled to hear him say, "This book has never been written." I asked him to explain, "To my knowledge, with all the books written on revival, none has ever attempted to write a theology of God's manifest presence." I was awestruck by Mr. Robert's words. He explained to us that most revival books are written sociologically, documenting the benefits of revival to society and the impact that God's manifest presence has had in the flow of human history. There were other books that documented sermons on revival. Yet there was none that provided a biblical foundation for the manifest presence of God.

In my former book, *Prayer on Fire*, I focused on the activity we need to employ in order to encounter the fire of God's manifest presence. In *God on Fire* I will focus on God's activity in encountering us. Since God always goes first, it is only appropriate that we shift our focus to Him.

In some ways, your generation has been ripped off. You've been lied to. Therefore, my goal is to prove from both Bible history and modern history that encountering *God on fire* is, or should be, the normal, daily, Christian experience. It is not the latest fad nor is it a passing fancy. God's manifest presence is here to stay. I hope to show that while the reality of *God on fire* is not new, it is something for every believer in Christ to experience now. It cannot remain in some archaeological museum or in the catacombs of church history. God desires to usher us into a fresh encounter with Himself, the manifest presence of Christ.

My other books taught people how to encounter God in prayer. This book is categorically different. Rather than starting with humanity, we will start with Deity. Even the very word "revival," as Roberts pointed out, is a word that starts with man, not God. God doesn't get revived; we do.

In case you didn't realize it, right now we are living in the middle of one of the most massive prayer movements in history. Around the world there are an estimated two hundred and ten million Christians who are praying for revival every day.[2] Twenty million of these believe that their primary calling in the body of Christ is to pray for revival.[3] There are also over ten million prayer groups in which people are praying for a coming world revival every time they meet.[4] The College of Prayer is one of thirteen hundred prayer mobilizing networks seeking to stir up the church to accelerate prayer for revival in world missions.[5] In Seoul, Korea, more than a million believers gathered in one place for an entire day of prayer in 1974.[6] On the Global Day of Prayer, celebrated each year on Pentecost Sunday, more than forty million believers gather in groups all over the world, crying out to God for a fresh Pentecost.

We find ourselves in the middle of a global tidal wave—a tsunami of a prayer movement. All these prayers are like heat-seeking missiles, locked in on the heat source of *God on fire*. Our prayers will not be denied, because only God could mobilize a global prayer force like this. *This global prayer movement is rocketing toward the vortex of the manifest presence of Christ.*

My greatest desire is to consistently lead people to a fresh encounter with Christ, particularly those in the next generation. In every season of my life, my passion to know Christ has grown consistently. Yet I must say, I am more hungry and more desperate to encounter the manifest presence of Christ now than ever before.

This book is intended to be more of an appetizer than a full course meal. For your generation it's more of a primer on the subject of God's manifest presence instead of a comprehensive encyclopedia. I have many buddies in the trenches who love God's manifest presence as much as I do. Special thanks to my young friends Bill Hyer, Pete Cannizzaro, Jonathan Gulley, Steven Smith and Andy Beare, who not only read the manuscript but gave significant input in its refinement. My administrative assistant, Ann Langley, has been more than an efficient executive administrator, going far beyond the call of duty. With excellence she put in more overtime hours than any of us could calculate, assisting me in preparing the manuscript and all the while seeming to thoroughly enjoy the process. Thanks also to my world-class editor, Tracey Lewis-Giggetts.

I write this book with a vision.

On February 1, 1974, the papers read "Sao Paulo, Brazil, on Fire." The upper floors of the largest investment bank in Latin America had caught on fire, and 188 people had died.

The day was September 2, 1949. The papers read "Chungking, China, on Fire." The riverfront docks had caught on fire, killing 1,700 people.

It was December 7, 1946. The papers read "Atlanta on Fire." The Winecoff Hotel at the corner of Ellis and Peachtree Streets had caught on fire, and 119 people had died.

The year was 1942. The papers read "Boston on Fire." In fifteen minutes a fire had ripped through the Coconut Grove Hotel, killing 492 people. It was the second-most deadly fire in U.S. history.

In 1871 the papers read "Chicago on Fire." Two hundred fifty people had died. Almost one hundred thousand people had been left homeless. Property damages were estimated back then at 175 million dollars.

The year was 1666. The papers read "London on Fire." Before they put out the fire, almost half the city had burned to the ground!

The vision I have is that the newspapers will read once again: "Sao Paulo on Fire!" "Chungking on Fire!" "Atlanta on Fire!" "Boston on Fire!" "Chicago on Fire!" "London on Fire!" This time cities around the world will burn not with a fire that kills and destroys but with a fire that cleanses. Purifies. Empowers. This book is written with a vision that the fire of God's manifest presence will once again ignite the church of Jesus Christ around the world.

This book was birthed in me when I was a student much like yourselves, and God has been writing this book in me ever since. I was first thrown into the fire of God's manifest presence when I was a seventeen-year-old growing up in New Jersey. While yet in high school, I read about America's great awakenings. Later in college I took all the Bible classes I could in order to feed my hunger to encounter God. In graduate school I took every possible church-history elective on revival, and for my entire adult life I have been leading people to encounter the manifest presence of Christ, both as a pastor of a local church and as president of the College of Prayer International.

I have written eighteen other books, but without question this is the most important. Though it contains my best effort to put on paper what God has put in me, I still write with a healthy degree of holy trembling.

The truth is this: you are not sick of church; you're sick of church without fire. Well, I have good news—so is Jesus. For this reason, He put in you the loathing for the treadmill of empty religious activity that He has.

One of my favorite movies is *Raiders of the Lost Ark*. It was produced before your time by Steven Spielberg, one of the world's greatest film directors. The hero of the story, Dr. Henry Walker Jones Jr., a.k.a. Indiana Jones, risked life and limb to retrieve the Ark of the Covenant—the Ark that quite literally contained the manifest presence of God. The Ark was carefully encased in a wooden box, nailed shut and wheeled deep into the archives of the Smithsonian Institute along with thousands of other boxes that looked identical. How could they put something so remarkable in a gigantic warehouse? Much in the same way the manifest presence of Christ has been marginalized and placed deep in the archives of church history. It is now my joy and adventure to retrieve it. I can almost hear the Indiana Jones theme song playing in the background.

If *God on fire* is as real as I contend, then none of us have the right to marginalize it. As followers of Christ, we are not curators of archaeological ruins or worshipers of a dead Messiah. As we will discover, we are *flame holders* who carry the blazing fire of God's manifest presence. So come on, students! Get on your feet! We need you to join with the great revivalists of history, many of whom God set on fire as young adults. Did you know that the First Great Awakening in the U.S. started with young people? Students just like you, such as Zinzendorf in Germany, Evan Roberts in Wales, the Cambridge Seven in England and George Whitefield in the United States and Europe. You might not be familiar with these names yet, but every one of these individuals was used as a fire-starter revivalist when he was in his twenties.

God says, "Your young men will see visions" (Joel 2:28; Acts 2:17). This is your time! God says, "On my servants, both men and women, I will pour out my Spirit in those days, and they will prophesy" (Acts 2:18). This is no time for you to turn your back on the church. We need you to take the church where it needs to go. It's time for you to embrace *God on fire.*

I want to give you a passionate prayer song written by one of the great fire starters, William Booth, founder of the Salvation Army. It may have been written one hundred years ago, but it is a song we need to sing again—now more than ever.

> Thou Christ of burning, cleansing flame,
> Send the fire, send the fire, send the fire!
> Thy blood-bought gift today we claim,
> Send the fire, send the fire, send the fire!
> Look down and see this waiting host,
> Give us the promised Holy Ghost;
> We want another Pentecost,
> Send the fire, send the fire, send the fire!
>
> God of Elijah, hear our cry:
> Send the fire, send the fire, send the fire!
> To make us fit to live or die,
> Send the fire, send the fire, send the fire!

To burn up every trace of sin,
To bring the light and glory in,
The revolution now begin,
Send the fire, send the fire, send the fire!

'Tis fire we want, for fire we plead,
Send the fire, send the fire, send the fire!
The fire will meet our every need,
Send the fire, send the fire, send the fire!
For strength to ever do the right,
For grace to conquer in the fight,
For pow'r to walk the world in white,
Send the fire, send the fire, send the fire!

To make our weak hearts strong and brave,
Send the fire, send the fire, send the fire!
To live a dying world to save,
Send the fire, send the fire, send the fire!
Oh, see us on Thy altar lay
Our lives, our all, this very day;
To crown the off'ring now we pray,
Send the fire, send the fire, send the fire!

Wake up! God Is Burning!

The sobering truth is that the greatest hindrance to the growth of
Christianity in today's world is the absence of the
manifest presence of God from the Church.[7]
Richard Owen Roberts

Our God is a consuming fire.
Hebrews 12:29

WE were made to go after God—full throttle, whole-hearted, all in. What we may not realize is that God
is pursuing us, and He is even more all in than we are. He is
more white-hot zealous to reveal Himself to us than we are to
know Him. God is certainly eternal, immortal and invisible.
He is also self-revealing. In other words, it is just as true to
God's nature to reveal Himself to His people as it is for Him
to be incognito. *God on fire* is when the invisible God chooses
to make known His presence to us in tangible ways. Can you
imagine the God of the universe communicating His presence
to you in unmistakable ways? This is not just a possibility. God
wants to make His fire a daily reality.

God on fire is why you and I were born. We are more alive
in the middle of God's white-hot presence than anywhere
else on earth. From the Garden of Eden, where humankind
walked with God in the cool of the day, to the final city where

God will dwell with His people, God's eternal purpose is to reveal Himself to us without interruption. The Bible is full of all-stars whose lives were marked by fire.

The All-Stars

Moses came alive when he met *God on fire*. He lived in obscurity on the back side of the desert, until one day God showed up in a burning bush, and Moses' life would never again be the same (see Exod. 3:2).

Abraham met *God on fire*. He'd heard God's voice before, but it wasn't until the day he saw the vision of the smoking firepot and the blazing torch that he knew God had made a covenant with him, and from that encounter everything would be different (see Gen. 15:17).

King David met *God on fire*. At a defining moment in his life, David sought the Lord, built an altar and sacrificed an animal, and while he was praying, God's fire fell from heaven and consumed not only his offering but his apprehensions (see 1 Chron. 21:26).

King Solomon met *God on fire*. At the dedication of the temple, he offered thousands of animals in sacrifice to God, knelt in prayer and lifted his hands to heaven, and while he was still worshiping, the fire of God fell and consumed the offering. No one was able to move or even lift a finger because the presence of God was so thick (see 2 Chron. 7).

Isaiah came alive when he met *God on fire*. He saw the Lord, heard the angels crying "Holy, holy, holy" at such a high decibel level that he could feel the footers of the temple shake. He responded the only way he knew how—by falling on his face and crying for mercy. An angel took a flaming coal from the presence of God and touched it to Isaiah's lips. The encounter with God defined Isaiah's life from that point forward (see Isa. 6).

All Israel met *God on fire*. When they were led through the wilderness by the pillar of cloud by day and the pillar of fire by night, they knew God was with them (see Exod. 13:21–22). When Moses received the ten Laws of God on the mountain, the Israelites were petrified that the entire mountainside was covered with fire (Exod. 19:16–19), but they again knew that God was with them.

The apostle Paul met *God on fire.* When Christ first appeared to him as Saul in a blinding flash of light on his way to Damascus, God spoke those defining words, "Saul, Saul, why do you persecute me? . . . I am Jesus" (Acts 9:4–5). On that day not only Paul's life but the course of history was changed by the fire of God's tangible presence.

The apostle John met *God on fire.* The risen, exalted, reigning Christ appeared to John in such high-definition clarity that John, who had seen Him a thousand times before, fell flat on his face like a dead man. It was as if Jesus was on fire from head to toe. This defining moment led John to write the final book in the Bible, the book of the Revelation. Because this book provides the clearest view of the exalted Christ, I will draw heavily from it as I uncover more about the manifest presence of God.

The early church came alive when they met *God on fire.* On the day of Pentecost, all the believers were not only filled with the Holy Spirit, they were clothed with flames of fire that wrapped around their heads (see Acts 2:3).

That is a lot of fire!

It's only the beginning.

In each of these examples, when people encountered the manifest presence of God, they knew it. No exceptions. No one was left wondering, *Was that really God?* No one was confused over what God was saying. For each of them, the encounter was a defining moment. A game-changer. The normally invisible God made Himself visible in His flaming presence, and these people's lives were never again the same.

Did you notice as well that in each of these *God on fire* moments, God was the focus, not the fire? None of these people obsessed over the fire. None began to worship or memorialize fire. They realized that fire (or clouds or crying angels) was the means by which God chose to communicate with them and not an end in itself.

It is important to keep in mind that most often the manifest presence of God will *not* be accompanied by fire—at least not literal fire. The critical issue is not the presence of fire but the presence of God. Because God is the ultimate creative genius and full of surprises, there are unlimited ways for Him to reveal His presence to us. Regardless of how He chooses to do so, it is important for us to keep our focus on Him and not on the manifestation.

My First Fire

I was first introduced to the fire of God's manifest presence in a friend's basement while listening to Bob Dylan music. In my earlier book *Prayer on Fire*, I told the story of how my friend asked a harmless and unexpected question: "You wanna pray?" He immediately dropped to his knees and, before I could answer, started to pray. How could I say no? I followed his lead and jumped right in. During the next forty-five minutes, God filled the basement with an overwhelming sense of His holiness. It was real. I had become a Christian a couple years prior to this, but my prayers had been predictable, routine, even boring. In a phrase, God seemed distant. I prayed because I was supposed to. This night, however, was refreshingly different. I felt alive. The experience was both relevant and invigorating.

What I did not share in *Prayer on Fire* is that a month after that incident, the fire of God's presence came to my local church in Chatham, New Jersey. It started with forty high school and college-aged students, myself included. As we began to pray one night, God showed up. We all became gut-check honest. We admitted to deception, hypocrisy and cover up. Confessions of cheating on tests, disobedience to parents, immorality, under-aged and excessive alcohol drinking, gossip, envy, jealousy and hatred flooded the space. We came clean that night, and in the days to come, we made things right. In my traditional church, for the first and perhaps only time, students ran down the center aisle of our sanctuary during Sunday evening worship to confess sin to their parents. We forgave, hugged and reconciled with each other. Families were healed, marriages were mended, and lives were changed forever. When I recently revisited my home church some thirty years later, many old friends reminded me of the time when God's presence visited our church.

That night ruined me. God's presence so rocked my world that once I tasted the goodness of His manifest presence and feasted my eyes on His glory, I never wanted to settle for anything less.

More Than Omnipresence

The omnipresence of God is a profound reality. It means that He is everywhere-at-the-same-time present. He promises to be with us always (see Matt. 28:20). He assures us that He will never leave us nor forsake us (see Josh. 1:9). It is impossible to get away from His Spirit or flee from His omnipresence (see Ps. 139:7–8). God's omnipresence benefits all people equally: Hindus, Buddhists, Muslims, Jews, secularists and atheists as well as Christians. You can't get any more or less of His omnipresence, nor can you alter your proximity to it. For this reason the omnipresence of God requires no prayer. Everyone on the planet benefits from the omnipresence of God in countless ways, and yet sadly, most people are clueless.

The manifest presence of God, however, is different. By its very definition, God's manifest presence is impossible to miss. Unlike the omnipresence, God's manifest presence is selective and highly personal. When Moses met *God on fire* in the burning bush, he was introduced to the manifest presence of God. He had walked by that bush a dozen times. While the omnipresence of God had been there all along, Moses did not recognize God's presence until God chose to make Himself conspicuously known.

The omnipresence and the manifest presence of God are both biblical and real, but there is a Grand Canyon difference between the two. A.W. Tozer was a forerunner in many ways. In his classic treatise *The Pursuit of God* he explains: "The presence and the manifestation of the presence are not the same. There can be one without the other. God is here when we are wholly unaware of it. He is manifest only when and as we are aware of His presence."[8]

As we dive deeper into God's manifest presence, we will gain far more clarity in distinguishing it from God's omnipresence. It may be helpful right now to compare and contrast the distinctives:

Omnipresence	Manifest Presence
Biblical	Biblical
Real	Real
True to God's nature	True to God's nature
God is everywhere	God is tangibly perceived
Generally theoretical	Generally transformational
Available to all	Normally for God's people
Universal	Selective
Absolutely no prayer required	Normally prayer required
Generally impersonal	Highly personal
Abstract	Specific
Obedience rare	Obedience required

The greatest tragedy in the church today is that we have confused the distinction between God's omnipresence and His manifest presence. God's purpose is for the flame of His manifest presence to be the power cell of the church. It is the single factor that distinguishes the church from the Kiwanis Club or the sports bar. The reason the church is in crisis today is because we have settled for the omnipresence rather than the manifest presence of God.

Because the church has not only blurred the distinction between the omnipresence and the manifest presence of God but has replaced one with the other, is it any wonder that we are in a crisis? Every month, one thousand five hundred pastors leave the ministry due to moral failure.[9] Seventy-five percent of pastors still in the ministry admit to a pornography habit.[10] Each year thirty-five hundred to four thousand churches close their doors, losing two million people to nominalism or secularism.[11] Why? Because the church has lost sight of its hallmark. We have forgotten our power cell.

The genius of the church is that God designed us to be the only human organization in which He promises to manifest His presence. Bill Hybels is right when he says the local church is the hope of the world. Let's quickly add, though, that the hope of the church is the manifest presence of Christ. Hybels also reminds us, "The future of the church rests primarily in the hands of its leaders.[12] " What we need today are pastors who not only provide effective leadership but who will shepherd the church back to a fresh encounter with the manifest presence of Christ. The church was born in the fire of the upper room on Pentecost; it was also born for the fire. The church thrives in the fire. There is nothing more wearisome, pointless or boring than trying to carry out church life without the fire. The real crisis is not that people are leaving the church every day by the thousands. The real crisis is that these same people were once in church and yet never encountered *God on fire*.

When Jesus said, "For where two or three come together in my name, there am I with them" (Matt. 18:20), He was not talking about God's omnipresence. God's omnipresence is there when people gather in the name of Mohammed or Buddha or David Letterman. Jesus was referring to God's manifest presence, because the there-am-I-with-them of Jesus is the hallmark, the power cell, the distinguishing feature that sets us apart as Christians. To miss this distinction is to completely miss the mark.

Rediscovering the reality of *God on fire* and the tangible presence of Christ in the church is a matter of life and death. We are not talking about roasting marshmallows around a little campfire or throwing a few logs in the fireplace to make our living room a bit cozier. We are talking about the raging inferno of God's tangible presence. We don't need a pep talk; we need an encounter.

Just One Problem

You and I share something in common. We were born with a capacity to know God. Buried down deep in our chest cavity is the innate ability to know Him. Like having an app that has never been activated, we have a capability to feast our eyes on God's glory that lies beneath our race, our religion, our ethnicity and even our sexual orientation. We were made for more than time; we were made for eternity.

There is just one problem. This capacity is buried, because it is dead. Like a still-born baby, the capacity is inside us, but it is dead and in need of resurrection. Fortunately, our God specializes in raising the dead. All it takes is one word from the mouth of God: *Hear! Behold! Fire! Arise!* Once God speaks to us, all bets are off. Everything instantly changes.

God's words are catalytic. At the voice of God, our *fire app* is instantly activated, and we are capable of receiving God's transmissions. What was previously dead is now alive. What was non-existent now exists.

God on fire is rooted first in God's nature and secondly in ours. He is the self-revealing God, and He loves to manifest His presence. As our forerunner friend A.W. Tozer said, "The pursuit of God is successful just because He is forever seeking to manifest Himself to us."[13] God will assist us in the process of knowing Him, because it is in Him to do so.

Even as I write, I am acutely aware of the utter futility of any attempt on my part to communicate the manifest presence of Christ and the reality of *God on fire*. Unless God sets on fire the words of this book, it will not happen. The only hope you and I have to encounter or even comprehend the fire of God is for God to take the paper-thin membrane that separates heaven and earth and to tear it in half. Remember, we are dead. Our ability to know God is dead. We need God to work a miracle inside us. We need Him to activate our receptors so that we are capable of detecting His presence. As Henry Blackaby said, "You never discover truth: truth is revealed. When the Holy Spirit reveals truth to you, He is not leading you into an encounter with God. That is an encounter with God."[14]

Every person who becomes a God-seeker has experienced three miracles:

1. The self-revealing God has chosen to make Himself known. That's a miracle.
2. God raised from the dead his or her ability to know Him. That's a miracle.
3. God put in that person a desire to seek Him. That's a miracle.

Receiving

The ability to receive is the key to encountering the manifest presence of God. When the hunger in our belly for God's manifest presence begins to increase, God wants to heal our receptors. He calls us to move beyond asking to receiving. For me it began with a rebuke: "Fred, your receiver is broken," God told me. I knew immediately what He meant. I was going through the motions and getting in proximity to God, but I was not receiving from Him. For months, whenever I'd pray, God would say to me, "Cup your hands. Hold out your hands to Me. Palms up in a posture to receive." It felt awkward at first. It insulted my self-sufficiency; my independence. God persisted, "Cup your hands!" Then an avalanche of Bible verses flooded my mind:

Ask and you will receive. (John 16:24)

Whoever does not receive the kingdom of God as a little child will by no means enter it. (Mark 10:15, nkjv)

Whatever things you ask in prayer, believing, you will receive. (Matt. 21:22, nkjv)

You will receive power. (Acts 1:8)

Receive the Holy Spirit. (John 20:22)

A man can receive nothing unless it has been given to him from heaven. (John 3:27, nkjv)

Come boldly to the throne of grace, that we may obtain mercy and find grace. (Heb. 4:16, nkjv)

Holding out our hands to God in a receiving posture is obviously not a religious ritual; it is a physical act declaring that we are responding to God's invitation to come and receive from Him. For a generation well-schooled in the significance of body language, we should be able to understand the benefits of extending our open hands to God in prayer. This physical gesture is not wishful thinking. It is an expression of our living faith in the living God.

When God chooses to manifest His presence, He is never arbitrary or careless. He always prepares His people in advance. Jesus told His disciples to not throw pearls before swine (see Matt. 7:6), and there is no finer pearl than the manifest presence of God. For this reason part of the prevenient, preparatory work of God is to first give us a holy hunger, followed by a desire to pray. The prayer that comes from that desire is a heart cry, a desperation, a burden, a groaning, a longing and, often, a need to ask. In the economy of God, don't underestimate the role of asking. Even more importantly, don't underestimate the role of receiving.

We certainly don't want to be theorists when it comes to God's presence. Instead, we want to be practitioners! So right now, let's ask Him to do what only He can do.

Father God, work a miracle in me. Rend the heavens and come down. Anoint this book with the oil of Your Spirit and set it on fire. Show up as I read. Take Your rightful place on center stage and sweep the dance floor clean. Take the wax out my ears that I might hear Your voice. Do cataract surgery on my eyes so I can see Your face. Open my chest cavity, take out my heart of granite and give me a heart of flesh with nerve endings that can feel and discern Your activity. Send the fire of Your manifest presence to consume the wood, hay and stubble of my stale religious routine. Remove the cobwebs from my prayer life. Reveal to me the glory of Your only Son, the Lord Jesus Christ.

The good news is that God knows how to speak our language. There is no one-size-fits-all when it comes to God's manifest presence. He knows how to uniquely manifest His presence in a way that each of us will clearly understand. The following list contains just a few of the many ways God may choose to manifest Himself to you:

answers to prayer	agreement in prayer
Bible verses He applies	prophecy
visions	miracles
dreams	divine appointments
sensory impressions (feelings, smells, sounds, sights)	Bible promises
healings	conviction of sin
counsel	repentance
words of wisdom and knowledge	reconciliation
tongues and interpretation	deliverance

As implied earlier in our list of Bible all-stars, *God on fire* is nothing new. It is as old as Adam, and it is far more conspicuous throughout history than one might realize. Christians through the ages have used various names for the fire of God's manifest presence. Jonathan Edwards, a leader of the 1746 Great Awakening, called it "Holy Spirit effusions."[15] Fifty years earlier the German Pietists referred to it as the "dwelling of God with men."[16] Reformer Ludwig Nicholas Von Zinzendorf was speaking from experience when he called it "our Pentecost."[17] During the Welsh revival people called it "the fire zone."[18] The young Evan Roberts, one of the leaders in the Welsh revival, called it "the divine fire."[19] Others in Wales said, "Glory filled the land."[20] In Southern India in 1905, people said, "God has come."[21] William Seymour of the Azusa Street Revival and the father of modern Pentecostalism not surprisingly called it "Pentecost."[22] Many simply use one word: revival.

The root of the word "revival" is vɪv, which means *life*, as in *vivid, vivacious* or *viva!* The prefix is *RE*, or *again*. Revival means to come to life again. As Welsh preacher Christmas Evans said, "Revival is God bending down to the dying embers of a fire just about to go out and breathing into it until it bursts into flame."[23] The real issue, of course, is not what we call it; the issue is, *do we have it?* Or, even more importantly, *do we want it?*

If you are tired of your all-too-familiar religious routine and want to encounter the manifest presence of Christ, welcome to *God on fire*.

In our journey, we will discover many truths about God, and even a few surprises:

- How does God reveal Himself?
- What does this tell us about God's nature?
- How can I be sure it is God?
- How do I recognize God's voice?

In light of what we learn about God, we will discover a few things about ourselves as well:

- How can I get dramatic answers to specific prayer?
- How can I discern between the counterfeit and the authentic?
- How can I see more of the supernatural power of God in my life and my family?
- How can I become more conscious of God's tangible presence in my daily life?

As much as I have encountered the manifest presence of *God on fire* over the past forty years and have hundreds of stories to report, the purpose of this book is not so much to

focus on the dramatic impact that God's manifest presence
has on people as it is to focus on God's manifest presence
itself. I will, however, end each chapter with one of the many
stories from church history. Garth Rosell, professor of church
history at one of the leading evangelical seminaries in the
United States, has compiled a revival bibliography of more
than twenty-six pages. Richard Owen Roberts has published
his list of revival books in a whopping 567-page volume. Of
all the narratives from church history from which to draw in
these volumes, I will include a single glimpse of revival from
history as we conclude each chapter. Hopefully you will feel
the heat.

God on Fire in History

Let me introduce you to Count Nicholas Ludwig Von
Zinzendorf. Don't let his unusual name distract you. On August
13, 1727, he, along with two hundred people, was gathered
for prayer and worship. When God's presence visited this
group, weeping, repentance, transparency, humility, confession
followed. Most of all, each believer was overwhelmingly
conscious of God's unmistakable manifest presence. They
met *God on fire* and would always mark that moment as their
Pentecost. The people were baptized with the Holy Spirit, and
dramatic signs and wonders were followed by deep confession
of sin. "The whole place was, indeed, a veritable dwelling of
God with men; and on the thirteenth of August it passed
into continual praise," Zinzendorf wrote.[24] Prayer and serious
devotion to Christ would characterize this group's fellowship
from that moment on.

Five years later, their first two missionaries were sent out.

As these two obeyed the missionary call, Zinzendorf charged them, "You are not to aim at the conversion of whole nations. You must simply look for seekers after the truth who like the Ethiopian eunuch seem ready to embrace the Gospel." Hundreds of missionaries would follow. For the first one hundred years, every Moravian missionary was a tentmaker, not taking one penny for his salary or services but rather earning his money while serving in foreign lands.[25]

Zinzendorf grew up in Germany in the early 1700s, and he encountered God's blazing presence many times during his childhood. "In my fourteenth year I began to seek God earnestly," he wrote, "and determined to become a true servant of Jesus Christ."[26]

He enrolled in the University of Halle, where he became a leader on campus and prayed desperately for missions and for unreached people around the world. He formed *The Order of the Mustard Seed* for fellow students who were seeking to lead people to faith in Christ and to practice acts of kindness. Their motto was "His wounds, our healing." Each member wore a ring inscribed with the words "No man lives to himself." Zinzendorf went on to further study at Wittenberg, where he started all-night prayer meetings for the nations.

Following graduation, Zinzendorf chose to invest his considerable wealth into providing a place of refuge for the religiously persecuted in Herrnhut, Germany. Zinzendorf called for extended times of God-encountering prayer. As Andrew Murray observed, "As at Pentecost, so at Herrnhut, united prayer, rewarded with the gift of the Spirit, was the entrance into the life of witness and victory. It is the law of all mission work."[27]

Their encounter with God's manifest presence was so compelling, so transforming, that it began a non-stop prayer meeting, twenty-four hours a day, seven days a week, that lasted one hundred years. During this time the Moravians sent out over six hundred missionaries worldwide. Those who study missions and mission work refer to this as the birth of the modern missionary movement. It all started with the God-encountering prayers of the righteous into which God poured the flaming reality of His manifest presence.[28]

Chapter Takeaways

- *God on fire* is why you and I were born.
- The Bible is full of all-stars whose lives were marked by fire.
- Often the manifest presence of God will not be accompanied by fire.
- The critical issue is not the presence of fire but the presence of God.
- God knows how to speak our language.

Are you ready to jump right into the furnace as we look at the blazing reality of the risen, exalted, triumphant Christ? To prepare yourself, you may want to grab your Bible and thoughtfully read the action-packed, mind-boggling first chapter of the final book in the Bible, the book of the Revelation.

The Revelation of Jesus Christ

Revival begins with a vision, and the vision begins with a new
sense of Jesus Christ. Revival does not begin in a theology, but in a
theophany. It begins in a revelation of Jesus Christ Himself and
a sense of the nearness of the Master.[29]
Charles Spurgeon

On the Lord's Day I was in the Spirit,
and I heard behind me a loud voice like a trumpet.
Revelation 1:10

WIPE your eyes. Now blink hard. You cannot imagine
what you are about to see. It's the risen, exalted,
enthroned, triumphant Christ. It is all captured in the first
chapter of the book of the Revelation. Stephen Spielberg,
George Lucas and the greatest minds of Hollywood would be
hard pressed to reproduce such vivid description.

John had seen Jesus a thousand times. The two of them
had done almost everything together for three years—fished,
hiked, grilled out. Yet John was not prepared to see anything
like what he saw that day. He came face to face with the
ultimate manifest presence of God.

It all started on a Sunday. John the apostle was serving
time in isolation as a religious prisoner of Rome on the
remote island of Patmos, located off the coast of Greece in

the Aegean Sea. In the middle of God-encountering worship, Jesus snuck up behind John and blew His trumpet like reveille in a military barrack. John jumped out of his skin! He turned around, took one look—and his jaw dropped wide open. He couldn't believe his eyes. It was Jesus!

Apocalypse

The most accurate picture of what Jesus looks like today is clearly documented in the last book of the Bible, the book of the Revelation. The first words of the book plainly state, "The revelation of Jesus Christ," or as originally written in Greek, "the apocalypse of Jesus Christ." In our generation, the word *apocalypse* has become synonymous with the cataclysmic end of history. That is not its original meaning. *Apocalypse* means "revelation," "uncovering" or "revealing." This is similar to the release of a new music video or the introduction of the latest fashion trends on the runways of New York City. In the revelation of Jesus Christ, Jesus is both the subject and the object of the revelation; that is to say, He is the One doing the revealing, and He is the One being revealed. The apocalypse of Jesus Christ means that what was hidden has now gone public.

Feast your eyes on the picture of the risen Christ painted for us in the book of the Revelation:

- Jesus is wearing a robe reaching down to His feet like a wealthy man of distinction or a priestly king. (see Rev. 1:13)
- He has a gold sash around His chest, indicating royal dignity, wealth and prominence. (see Rev. 1:13)
- His head and hair are pure white, glowing with wisdom and honor. (see Rev. 1:14)
- His eyes are like flames of fire or laser beams,

able to cut through the steel-plated armor of our defense mechanisms, seeing past our hypocrisy and superficiality. (see Rev. 1:14)

- His feet are glowing like molten metal showing His endurance, perseverance and authority over adversity. (see Rev. 1:15)
- His voice sounds like the waves crashing upon the coastline; His words keep coming and coming and coming. (see Rev. 1:15)
- His right hand holds seven stars. Not tiny "twinkle, twinkle little stars" but gigantic masses of burning fuel. These stars represent the leaders of local churches and Christ's authority over them. (see Rev. 1:16)
- Out of His mouth comes a razor-sharp, three- to five-foot sword, representing the power of His words, cutting and penetrating as the Word of God. (see Rev. 1:16)
- He is walking in the middle of seven flame holders that correspond to the seven local churches. (see Rev. 1:12–13)
- His face? It glows with the intensity of the noonday sun shining in all its brilliance. (see Rev. 1:16)

It is no wonder that this revelation of Jesus was enough to knock John off his feet. He immediately hit the deck, facedown and spread-eagle. In his own words, "When I saw him, I fell at His feet as though dead" (Rev. 1:17). Think comatose. John was incinerated by the nuclear-meltdown fire of the manifest presence of God.

John was immediately struck by the jarring realization of what Jesus looked like in that moment. Jesus was no longer a baby lying in a manger. He was not the brutalized body dangling from the cross. Nor was He simply the Jewish rabbi, or good teacher, whom John had followed for three years as

His disciple. This was essentially the same man, and yet He wasn't. What John saw is the reality of what Christ looks like today.

Jesus is no longer traveling incognito. He will never again voluntarily lay aside the use of His divine attributes (see Phil. 2:6–8), He will not come to earth as a baby, nor will He be nailed to a tree. All authority in heaven and on earth has now been given to Him (see Matt. 28:18). He has conquered the enemies of sin, death and Satan. Jesus is the hero who has risen, has ascended and is exalted to the highest place. He is seated on the throne of the universe and given the highest name, King of kings and Lord of lords (see Phil. 2:9).

The imagery of Jesus' appearance might seem surrealistic or bizarre, but don't allow that to distract you from the clarity of the revelation. John wrote what he saw. He was not trying to be clever or poetic, randomly selecting word pictures to make Jesus appear like a Marvel Comics superhero or a Jedi knight. He was told, "Write on a scroll what you see" (Rev. 1:11), and that's exactly what he did. Since this is the clearest revelation of what Jesus looks like today, let's dig in a little deeper.

What is readily apparent is that Jesus is on fire from head to toe. His hands are on fire. His face is on fire. His eyes are on fire. His feet are on fire. He is literally on fire from head to toe! In addition to all that, Jesus is walking *in* the fire among the torches, or flame holders. Why all the fire? Simple. He is on fire because Jesus is the manifest presence of God. As we saw in the Bible all-star roll call, God frequently chooses to manifest His presence via fire. This image of Jesus on fire is rooted deeply in His nature, because He is the manifest presence of God.

This description is perfectly consistent with how Jesus is identified throughout the rest of the New Testament. When Christ was born, He was immediately recognized as Immanuel, God with us (see Matt. 1:23). He is, after all, the eternal

Word made flesh (see John 1:1) who dwells among us and communicates God's glory in a way we can each understand (see John 1:14). He is the image of the unseen God (see Col. 1:15), the exact representation of God's being (see Heb. 1:3), who can uniquely stand up and say, "To see Me is to see the Father" (see John 14:9).

Christ, the conquering hero, no sooner revealed Himself to His friend, John, when He immediately instructed him, "Write what you see." His intention was obvious. The revelation of Jesus Christ in all His glory was not intended purely for John. The revelation was to be written down for the seven local churches in John's day as well as for all of us throughout the ages. John's record is brimming with potent revelation into how and why God manifests His presence and how we should appropriately respond. Let's take a closer look into the first chapter of the book of Revelation. Read slowly. Reread. There is more biblical truth and practical theology in the next two pages than you may realize at first glance.

What We Discover about God

"*The revelation*" (1:1). God is a self-revealing God who loves to manifest His presence to His people. It starts with God, not with us. God always goes first. He initiates the process of revelation, and we respond to it.

"*The revelation of Jesus Christ*" (1:1). The unveiling of God is communicated through Christ. We only ever see the "light of the knowledge of the glory of God in the face of Christ" (2 Cor. 4:6). Every time God manifests Himself to us, He does so in and through His Son, Jesus.

"*I was in the Spirit*" (1:10). The Holy Spirit is the Person in the triune Godhead who does for us what we cannot do for ourselves: He reveals Christ. Because our capability of knowing God is dead and buried, it is the Holy Spirit who activates our ability to know God. He also activates our craving to know God. When we are *in the Spirit*, we are transformed from being people who have no desire for God to people who desire to know Him more than anything else in life.

"*Among the lampstands [flame holders]*" (1:13). Jesus walks among the flame holders, inspecting the fire of the manifest presence of God in every local church. The success of Christ's work on earth through the church depends on the brightness of the flame.

"*Eyes were like blazing fire . . . feet were like bronze glowing in a furnace . . . face was like the sun shining*" (1:14–16). The revelation of God's manifest presence is often communicated by fire—*God on fire.*

"*In his right hand he held seven stars*" (1:16). Not only is God Himself on fire, He holds the fire. He exercises dominion over His own reviving presence. He alone has sovereignty over His servants whom He ignites like flames of fire (see Heb. 1:7), and He empowers His servants to offer the fire of His presence to others.

What We Discover about Ourselves

"*I, John, your brother*" (1: 9). When God chooses to show Himself, He doesn't look for extraordinary people. He takes ordinary people like fishermen. Everyone is able to encounter God's manifest presence, including you.

"*I . . . was on the island of Patmos*" (1:9). When God chooses to manifest His presence, it can be anywhere at any time. He will often make Himself known in some of the least likely places. The apostle John met God first on a boat in the Sea of Galilee, then in the upper room in Jerusalem, and, now, on a remote island in the Aegean Sea.

"*A loud voice like a trumpet*" (1:10). God always goes first. He initiates the revelation of Christ, and we respond. When He gets our attention, His voice is always loud and invasive, even shocking, like a wake-up call out of a deep sleep. Remember, we have a serious problem—both our capability to know God and our craving to know Him are dead and buried. They need to be raised from the grave. The resurrection of our ability to know God happens the moment He sounds the trumpet, calls us by name or somehow tangibly makes Himself known.

"*I turned around*" (1:12). Encountering God always involves a turnaround. Repentance is a key part of the process of experiencing God.

"*When I saw him*" (1:17). There is nothing more riveting, more fulfilling, than feasting our eyes on the glory of God's manifest presence in the face of Jesus Christ. It is why we were born. More than simply being spellbinding or breathtaking, the manifest presence of God is transforming. It changes us. It thoroughly eclipses everything else in our lives.

"*I fell at his feet as though dead*" (1:17). The moment we encounter God, we are ruined. Life will never again be the same. There is nothing more humbling than coming face to face with Christ. If John the apostle, who was best friends with Jesus, who had laid his head on Jesus' shoulder, fell flat on the ground like a dead man in front of the exalted Christ, imagine what seeing Jesus will be like for the rest of us!

"*He placed his right hand on me*" (1:17). Our encounter with God is initially humbling, but it soon becomes empowering. Invigorating. Every person in the Bible whom God called to Himself received his or her life's calling and assignment in ministry from an encounter with God's manifest presence. The hand of Jesus on John's shoulder was the affirmation of John's call and the clarity of his assignment.

"*Do not be afraid*" (1:17). A genuine encounter with God delivers us from destructive and inappropriate fears that make us want to run and hide from the Lord. We receive instead a healthy respect for God that makes us want to serve, obey, love and follow Him. We throw off the spirit of religious slavery and receive the spirit of adoption—becoming a son or daughter of God.

Wake Up!

The book of the Revelation includes a wake-up call. "On the Lord's Day I was in the Spirit," John wrote, "and I heard behind me a loud voice like a trumpet" (Rev. 1:10). The trumpet blast was necessary to get John's undivided attention and to prepare him for an awesome encounter. The trumpet blast alerted him to the reality of the manifest presence of God in Christ and the significant place of Christ's presence in John's life and in the life of the early church.

The manifest presence of Christ is the essence of the church—the very reason for its existence. If John and the early church needed to be refocused, realigned and revived, we certainly do too. God intended to establish for all time the purpose of the church's existence: to receive and hold out like flame holders the manifest presence of Christ. *God on fire* was never intended to be a rare occurrence or a distant memory. *God on fire* should be a consistent reality for the church throughout the ages. The lamp stands Jesus walked among were not just clever word pictures holding sentimental, nostalgic value. They were making a prophetic statement of the role and reality of the local church for all time.

God is blowing another trumpet in our generation. He is awakening people today to the reality of His manifest presence and its magnitude in our life and in the life of the church in the twenty-first century. The modern church has become preoccupied and distracted with activity, technology and methodology. We desperately need a wake-up call to alert us to the reality of God's manifest presence and to lead us into a fresh encounter with Him.

The bottom line is this: Jesus is the manifest presence of God. Because we are God seekers and not manifestation seekers, we always want to keep our eyes on Christ. Once we fully grasp the reality that Christ is the One who communicates God to us and that every authentic manifestation is an expression of Himself, doors will not only open to the supernatural, but we will also be empowered to avoid excess. As we develop a healthy biblical theology of the reviving presence of God, we will always build on the foundational cornerstone of Christ.

So take one more good and hard look at the portrait of Jesus found in the first chapter of the book of the Revelation. Before you close the book or turn the page, close your eyes and reflect on Jesus, the manifest presence of God. Picture Him standing before you as He stood before John. Jesus is ablaze with fire—the fire of the manifest presence of God. He is glowing with the knowledge of the glory of God. Yes, you could travel the world and see the most breathtaking sights. But I can assure you, there is nothing on this earth that will compare with seeing the glory of God.

> *Exalted Jesus, awaken me to Your manifest presence. Blow the trumpet in my soul. Sound the alarm! Raise from the dead my capacity to know You. I cry out for apocalypse! Unveiling! Uncovering! Reveal Yourself to me. I want to see the light of the knowledge of the glory of God shining in the face of Jesus Christ. Today. Tomorrow. Always.*

God on Fire in History

It's unfortunate, but St. Patrick is usually only remembered along with shamrocks, leprechauns and tall drafts of beer. History has all but forgotten that he forgave his tormentors, healed the sick and converted the king of England. Patrick was a mighty man of prayer who had a significant influence on Scotland, England and other nations of the world.

Patrick became a follower of Christ as a young man. Through a dream God called him to be a missionary in to Ireland, the land in which, during his youth, he had spent four years as a slave. He was obedient to God's call and went back to preach the grace and forgiveness of God to his former tormentors. What he lacked in formal theological training God gave him in zeal, power and love. As a result, his ministry profoundly impacted the course of history in Ireland and in the British Isles. Patrick's humble, transparent and straightforward manner won the respect of the people as he fearlessly confronted the popular Druid idolatry of his day.

On one occasion a Druid magician, Lochru, cursed God while Patrick was praying. Patrick refused to be intimidated, and as he continued to pray, Lochru was supernaturally lifted into the air and thrown to the ground.[30] Following the dramatic encounter, it is reported that King Leogaire (pronounced "Leery") of England repented and came to faith in Christ, opening all of Ireland to the gospel.

Patrick performed many other miracles, wrote hymns and led revivals for thirty years. Some historians estimate that he started three hundred sixty-five churches and led over one hundred twenty thousand people to salvation in Christ.[31]

Before using St. Patrick God dramatically demonstrated His manifest presence through Gregory of the Nazianzos in 205 AD. Gregory converted to Christ at age twenty-nine and was used of God to perform many miracles, healings and casting out of demons. He could move stones with a verbal command and even stop the overflow of rivers. Each of these works of power was influential in leading people to faith in

Christ. Gregory became known as Gregory the Wonder-worker and was officially named Bishop of Neo-Caesarea.[32]

And further back than Gregory, Irenaeus called the church in his day to repentance, holiness and revival. He was born in Asia Minor about 130 AD and became a third-generation Christian and disciple of Polycarp. He wrote in his own words, "How Polycarp had received them from eye-witnesses of the Word of Life. . . . I listened eagerly even then to these things through the mercy of God which was given to me, and made notes of them, not on paper but in my heart."[33]

Irenaeus wrote the five-volume revival treatise entitled *Against Heresies* in or around 185 AD. These books refuted Gnosticism and called believers to a fresh encounter with Christ. It became one of the most important documents of the early church.[34]

Each of these three—St. Patrick, Gregory the Wonder-worker and Irenaeus—were forerunners of the faith who encountered the reality of God's manifest presence.

Chapter Takeaways

- In the book of Revelation, Jesus is on fire from head to toe.
- Jesus Christ is the ultimate manifest presence of God.
- The manifest presence of Christ is the essence of the church.
- We are God-seekers and not manifestation-seekers.

When feasting the eyes on the manifest presence of God, there are only two options: We either turn away from God's invitation to encounter His manifest presence or we turn around and run into His arms. John, as we will see, made the right choice.

Am I Ignitable?

The prayer preceding all prayer is,
"May it be the real I who speaks.
May it be the real Thou that I speak to." [35]
C.S. Lewis

I heard behind me a loud voice like a trumpet.
Revelation 1:10

THE fact that anyone can encounter the manifest presence of God is more than remarkable; it is miraculous. Only when we realize that we are utterly incapable of recognizing God, even if He were to walk past us in broad daylight, will we truly appreciate the miracle. In fact, in Ephesians 2 the Bible tells us that we are spiritually dead. We can no more hear God's voice or see His face than a dead person in a casket can recognize those who attend his funeral.

There are four often debated perspectives on human nature:

1. People are by nature good.
2. People are basically good with a little evil.
3. People are evil with a little good.
4. People are by nature evil.

Which view of human nature is accurate? If *USA Today* or CNN were to conduct an opinion poll on these four viewpoints, what would the results show? It's hard to say, but I'm quite certain the first three options would score well. Yet God's perspective is radically different from ours.

When God originally created humankind in His image—to be a reflection of His nature and to enjoy His presence—humanity was in category one: by nature good. However, humanity turned its back on God and dived into spiritual death. We fell from category one to category four. As unflattering as it sounds, for an accurate reflection on what humanity looks like from God's perspective, check out the following descriptions from His Word:

There is no one righteous, not even one. (Rom. 3:10)

There is no one who understands, no one who seeks God. (Rom. 3:11)

All have turned away. (Rom. 3:12)

For all have sinned and fall short of the glory of God. (Rom. 3:23)

But your iniquities have separated you from your God; your sins have hidden his face from you, so that he will not hear. (Isa. 59:2)

Their feet rush into sin; they are swift to shed innocent blood. Their thoughts are evil thoughts; ruin and destruction mark their ways. (Isa. 59:7)

All have turned aside, they have together become corrupt; there is no one who does good, not even one. (Ps. 14:3)

Just as a patient visiting a doctor wants an accurate account of his condition despite how disturbing the account may be, we also stand before God to receive an accurate diagnosis of our problem. The best part of visiting Dr. Jesus is that He has everything required to heal our illnesses.

The Fall

When Adam and Eve chose to disobey God, they did more than stub their toes; they fell down, face first. The Fall did major damage to our disposition toward the manifest presence of God. The omnipresence of God, on the other hand, was not impacted by the Fall at all. God was everywhere prior to sin entering the world, and He remains everywhere today. The main difference in our relationship to God following the Fall is that sin drove a wedge between humanity and the manifest presence of God. A shift took place within the human spirit. Like a gigantic earthquake that left us out of alignment at our core, our entire disposition was altered so that rather than crave God's presence, we now want to run and hide. The days of being naked and unashamed have been replaced with fig leaves and cover-ups. Hypocrisy and pretending have become second nature. Prior to the Fall, Adam and Eve were free to be themselves, because the manifest presence of God created a safe environment in which they could thrive. Turning their backs on His presence, however, plunged them into the deception of cover-up, masquerade and deception. They found themselves playing a part rather than being true to themselves. This same charade is played out throughout history whenever people lose contact with the manifest presence of God.

A shallow view of human depravity is one of the primary sources of bad theology. It is called Pelagianism and is named after a fifth-century heretic named Pelagius. His view of human nature waffled between the second and third viewpoints of human nature noted earlier in this chapter: that people are basically good with a little evil or that people are evil with a little good. Augustine, a theologian and one of the greatest Christian thinkers of all time, confronted Pelagius head on and helped the church confront the other heresies that grew out of this shallow view of sin.

The Brainstem

Many of us grew up in churches where they *have* a revival rather than *pray* for one. It is as if revivals are man-made rather than God-made. Church marquees read, "Revival this Sunday through Wednesday," as if we can turn revivals on and turn them off. This distorted view risks crossing the line and touching the sovereignty of God. It is rooted in a shallow view of human depravity. So where did this bad thinking come from? It is rooted in age-old Pelagianism, and it was popularized by none other than Charles Finney.

Charles Finney lived during a massive, sixty-year revival in American history that occurred primarily in the New England states. From 1792 to 1848, there was not a year without revival in New York state. Finney did not initiate the revival, but he certainly enjoyed the benefits. He saw some of the most extraordinary manifestations of God and was himself the recipient of many. "The Holy Spirit seemed to go through me, body and soul," he wrote. "I could feel the impact like a wave of electricity going through and through me. Indeed it seemed to come in waves of liquid [love.]" [36] While I will not discredit the authenticity of Finney's encounters with God, he is certainly not a role model for revival nor a good theologian. As my friend Richard Owen Roberts shared with me, "No one has done more damage to revival than Charles Finney." When I asked Mr. Roberts to clarify his strong criticism, he said, "Finney taught, 'If I ought, I can.' He taught the plant-acrop-and-get-a-revival approach." It seems as if Finney tried to reduce the sovereign work of God to a mere work of man.

In later writings Finney admitted he was wrong: "I have thought that, at least in a great many instances, stress enough has not been laid upon the necessity of Divine influence upon the hearts of Christians and sinners. I am confident that I have sometimes erred in this respect myself . . . I have laid, and I doubt not that others have also laid, too much stress on the natural ability of sinners, to the neglect of showing them the nature and extent of their dependence on the grace of God and the influence of His Spirit. This has grieved the Spirit of God."[37]

Tragically, in the latter years of his life, Finney saw no move of God. A shallow view of human depravity challenges the reality of all three miracles of divine revelation:

1. The miracle of God's self-revelation becomes unnecessary, because we pridefully think we can know God without His help.

2. The miracle of God giving us the capacity to know Him becomes unnecessary, again because we have the ability in and of ourselves.

3. The miracle of putting the desire within us to seek His face is also unnecessary if we can have the desire, or so we think, without any of God's intervention.

But the most tragic error of all is that a shallow view of human depravity challenges the core Christian doctrine of the sovereignty of God. The old theologians have referred to this fundamental, biblical truth of God's sovereignty as the brainstem of the Christian faith. It is the single doctrine that God is God, and we are not (see Ps. 115:1). To violate the sovereignty of God in revival and to reduce the manifest presence of God to a formula or a program is like touching the brainstem of faith. You don't touch the brainstem without killing the person, and you don't violate the sovereignty of God without jeopardizing the entire framework of your relationship with Him.

Since revival is of God's initiative and not our own, there are a few Kingdom-seeking, manifest-presence-encountering, *God on fire* principles that we want to clearly identify:

- God is a self-revealing God. No one will ever force his or her way into God's presence. Like a one-way mirror, God always sees us. We don't see Him until He turns on the light and gives us a glimpse into His glory.
- We are spiritually dead and utterly dependent on God not only to reveal Himself to us but to awaken our capacity to receive.
- Only God can activate in us the capability to know Him. Only He can empower us with the capacity to see, hear, recognize and discern His manifest presence.

Once God activates our capacity, He then arouses in us a craving to know Him. Hunger to know God is all by itself an awesome work of God. The Bible says, "No one . . . seeks God" (Rom. 3:11). When God activates our capacity and arouses our craving, He motivates in us a new desire to pray—to call on the Lord.

Healthy Hunger

Undoubtedly, hunger for God precedes an encounter with God. It is the fire in our belly that prepares us to encounter the fire of God's presence. As Martin Luther said, "Hunger is the best cook."[38] Hunger is miracle number one in a long sequence of chain-reaction miracles. It creates a spontaneous spiritual combustion that culminates with an encounter with *God on fire*. Hunger is the evidence of God's prevenient grace—a term theologians use to refer to the fact that God always goes first. Always.

Spiritual hunger and spiritual health go hand in hand. You do not have one without the other. As we have seen, it is not in us to naturally pursue God. There is no person who is a natural-born worshiper. There are no natural-born seekers and absolutely no natural-born hunger-ers. Not one. This means whenever we notice a desire deep down in our gut to seek God in prayer and worship, there is a sure-fire guarantee that God has something up His sleeve. He is setting in motion a God-encounter.

Because it is God-given, spiritual hunger is also God-fulfilled. You can bank on it. You do not ever need to worry about being ripped off by God. "No one whose hope is in [the Lord]," God says, "will ever be put to shame" (Ps. 25:3). "If you seek me, you will find me," God says (see Jer. 29:13). "Come near to God," again the Word of God promises, "and He will come near to you" (James 4:8). The more you feed your spiritual hunger, the bigger it grows. Hunger for God can sit dormant for a while. If it goes unnoticed and unfed, it will not force a response. When God triggers our appetite alarm, He wants a reply. It's part of His wake-up call. God sovereignly does whatever He wants, and part of His sovereign activity is to call us to respond to His presence. Like a mother calling out to her children playing in the back yard during dinnertime, urging them to "Come and get it!" God invites us to come.

The Bible is full of examples of people who experienced God placing a world-class hunger inside their bellies. Jacob cried out, "I will not let you go unless you bless me" (Gen. 32:26). Moses cried, "If your Presence does not go with us, do not send us up from here" (Exod. 33:15). King David said, "As the deer pants for streams of water, so my soul pants for you, O God" (Ps. 42:1). David also announced, "One thing I ask of the LORD, this is what I seek: that I may dwell in the house of the LORD all the days of my life, to gaze upon the beauty of the LORD and to seek him in his temple" (Ps. 27:4). The apostle Paul groaned, "But one thing I do: Forgetting what is behind and straining toward what is ahead, I press on toward the goal to win the prize for which God has called me heavenward in Christ Jesus" (Phil. 3:13).

Wonder

When encountering the manifest presence of God, never fail to greet Him with wide-eyed wonder. Never cease to be amazed when He sovereignly chooses to manifest His presence, because each time He does, it is just as much a miracle as it was the first time. No one by exercising human intelligence, superior powers of reason or self effort will ever be capable of gaining a single glimpse of God. Not Bill Gates, one of the wealthiest men in the world. Not Stephen Hawking, one of the most intelligent men in the world. Even more, no one would ever *want* to gain a glimpse of God unless God put that desire within him or her. This is why we can never pride ourselves in our desire to seek God and pray and why we should be utterly overwhelmed with gratitude for the ability to know Christ, the desire to seek Him and the wonder of encountering Him. Because we—with all our intellectual and emotional faculties—are spiritually dead, we each need a loud-voice-like-a-trumpet moment.

He wakes us up out of our own casket so we can live again. "Wake up, O sleeper," God says, "rise from the dead, and Christ will shine on you" (Eph. 5:14). How does He awaken us? When God wakes us up out of our stupor, He awakens our spirit.

It requires a trumpet blast to move us from knowing about the *theoretical* presence of God to being able to recognize the manifest presence of God. When the flaming presence of Christ appeared to John, the apostle was already familiar with Christ. But this day was different. He awakened to a vision he'd never before seen. He saw dimensions of the character, virtue and personhood of Christ that were altogether new to him. He discovered a host of vital truths about the way God manifests Himself. When John turned around, he saw Christ in all His glory and fell on His face in sheer wonder.

Warning

When it comes to knowing Christ and encountering His manifest presence, don't dabble. Seek Him with reckless abandon. The world will never be changed by people who dabble. Don't settle for a superficial, arm-distant relationship. Turn around. Christ is calling you all in. Dabbling is an insult to God. Jesus was not mangled on the cross nor did he rise from the dead so that we might dabble. Since God is on fire, how could we dabble?

When King David took dominion over his own soul and commanded it at the top of his lungs, "Praise the Lord, O my soul; all my inmost being, praise his holy name" (Ps. 103:1), he was evicting dabbling from his heart. He was declaring zero tolerance on dabbling. When the white-hot God said to His people, "Love the Lord your God with all your heart and with all your soul and with all your strength" (Deut. 6:5), He left no room for dabbling. When Jesus commended His hostess, Mary, for her full-throttle worship and rebuked her uptight, stressed-out, older sister, Martha, He was plainly condemning unfocused worship – another form of dabbling. "'Martha,' the Lord answered, 'you are worried and upset about many things, but only one thing is needed. Mary has chosen what is better, and it will not be taken away from her'" (Luke 10:41–42).

The apostle Paul cleaned out his locker room of religious

hobbies and officially went on record: "No more dabbling; I want Jesus!" (see Phil. 3). Even Jesus in the book of the Revelation rebuked the church for dabbling: "I know your deeds, that you are neither cold nor hot. I wish you were either one or the other! So, because you are lukewarm—neither hot nor cold—I am about to spit you out of my mouth" (Rev. 3:15–16).

The sound technician at my church, a man with a pleasant sense of humor, came up to me after a sermon I preached on encountering the flaming presence of God and joked, "I realized while you were preaching this morning that when God one day commends us, He will not say *medium-rare* but *well done*, good and faithful servant!" That's exactly right!

Knowing the depth of our own depravity, every time we encounter the manifest presence of Christ, it is a miracle. Using the words of missionary martyr, Jim Elliott, right now let's ask God for this very miracle:

> *Am I ignitable? God deliver me from the dreaded asbestos of other things. Saturate me with the oil of your Spirit that I may be aflame. But flame is transient, often short-lived. Canst thou bear this, my soul-short life? In me there dwells the Spirit of Great Short-Lived whose zeal for God's house consumed him. And he has promised baptism with the Spirit and with the Fire. Make me thy fuel, Flame of God.*[39]

God on Fire in History

Dwight Lyman Moody was one of the most influential people of the mid-19th century. With minimal education, he preached to presidents and parliaments.

Close friend of Moody, R.A. Torrey, wrote the book *Why God Used D.L. Moody?* While the entire book is inspiring,[40] the clinching answer to his question is that Moody received the baptism of the Holy Spirit. "My heart was not in the work of begging. I could not appeal," he wrote describing Moody's own Spirit-baptism. "I was crying all the time that God would fill me with His Spirit. Well, one day, in the city of New York—oh, what a day!—I cannot describe it, I seldom refer to it; it is almost too sacred an experience to name."[41] Moody said, "I believe we should accomplish more in one week than we should in years if we had only this fresh baptism."[42]

Enjoy the powerful words of Torrey as he describes a most memorable encounter with God's manifest presence:

> I shall never forget the eighth of July, 1894, to my dying day. It was the closing day of the Northfield Students' Conference—the gathering of the students from the eastern colleges. Mr. Moody had asked me to preach on Saturday night and Sunday morning on the baptism with the Holy Ghost. On Saturday night I had spoken about, "The Baptism With the Holy Ghost: What It Is; What It Does; the Need of It and the Possibility of It." On Sunday morning I spoke on "The Baptism With the Holy Spirit: How to Get It." It was just exactly twelve o'clock when I finished my morning sermon, and I took out my watch and said: "Mr. Moody has invited us all to go up to the mountain at three o'clock this afternoon to pray for the power of the Holy Spirit. It is three hours to three o'clock. Some of you cannot wait three hours. You do not need to wait. Go to your rooms; go out into the woods; go to your tent; go anywhere where you can get alone with God and have this matter out with Him."

> At three o'clock we all gathered in front of Mr.

Moody's mother's house (she was then still living), and then began to pass down the lane, through the gate, up on the mountainside. There were four hundred and fifty-six of us in all; I know the number because Paul Moody counted us as we passed through the gate.

After a while Mr. Moody said: "I don't think we need to go any further; let us sit down here." We sat down on stumps and logs and on the ground. Mr. Moody said: "Have any of you students anything to say?" I think about seventy-five of them arose, one after the other, and said: "Mr. Moody, I could not wait till three o'clock; I have been alone with God since the morning service, and I believe I have a right to say that I have been baptized with the Holy Spirit."

When these testimonies were over, Mr. Moody said: "Young men, I can't see any reason why we shouldn't kneel down here right now and ask God that the Holy Ghost may fall upon us just as definitely as He fell upon the apostles on the Day of Pentecost. Let us pray." And we did pray, there on the mountainside. As we had gone up the mountainside heavy clouds had been gathering, and just as we began to pray those clouds broke and the raindrops began to fall through the overhanging pines. But there was another cloud that had been gathering over Northfield for ten days, a cloud big with the mercy and grace and power of God; and as we began to pray our prayers seemed to pierce that cloud and the Holy Ghost fell upon us. Men and Women, that is what we all need: the Baptism with the Holy Ghost.[43]

Moody loved university students. During several meetings he led at Cambridge, seventeen hundred cynical students would fill the lecture hall with the intention to mock and disrupt the presentation. They would laugh, pound sticks and ignite firecrackers. However, the students proved no match for the three hundred praying mothers Moody had recruited. The Holy Spirit came into those meetings, and a missionary force that would forever change the world marched out. God put His hand on the famous Cambridge Seven: Charles Thomas "C.T." Studd, Stanley P. Smith, Dixon Edward "D.E." Hoste and four other Cambridge University students. Each of them was converted to Christ that week during Moody's meetings and called into career missionary service. These seven students triggered what became the Student Volunteer Movement and ignited modern missions.

Chapter Takeaways

- The Bible tells us we are spiritually dead.
- The fact that anyone can encounter the manifest presence of God is a miracle.
- The biblical truth of God's sovereignty is the brainstem of the Christian faith.
- You don't touch the brainstem without killing the person.
- Hunger for God precedes an encounter with God.
- Never fail to greet God with wide-eyed wonder.

God has thought of everything. Knowing all our deficiencies, He has a solution to meet them head on. That being said, let's discover what God does to call us back to His manifest presence.

Turn Back to the Fire

Separation from the Presence is, quite literally, what the Fall *is*. As a result of the Fall, mankind slipped from God-consciousness into the hell of self and self-consciousness. [44]
Leanne Payne

I turned around to see the voice that was speaking to me.
Revelation 1:12

IT is no mere coincidence that when the apostle John heard the booming voice that sounded like a trumpet blast, he turned around. He had been pointed in the wrong direction! Humanity has collectively been pointing in the wrong direction for years. As we have seen, turning our backs on God's manifest presence dates all the way back to Adam and Eve.

Both man and woman, whom God created in His own image, at first enjoyed living in His manifest presence. They even walked around the garden with God in the cool of the day (see Gen. 3:8). However, after they consciously disobeyed God, they immediately, instinctively, did what they'd never done before: "They hid from the LORD God," we are told, "among the trees of the garden" (Gen. 3:8). When you think about it, hiding from God is pretty stupid. Nevertheless, at the point of Adam and Eve's sin, a new phenomenon came into play. It's called cover-up. For the first man and woman, reaching for fig leaves to cover their shame was like putting a small bandage on a large, gaping wound.

They didn't learn to cover up over time. They hadn't observed it in others. It came intuitively, like a gag reflex. This critical moment in mankind's history marked a line of demarcation. In that instant, humanity turned its back on God and began pointing in the wrong direction. Something deep inside the first couple's core had changed, and the consequences were far reaching. Hiding, masking and posing are now part of the human genome. Pretense and deceit are part of our makeup. Adam and Eve were obviously not hiding from the omnipresence of God, since that is impossible. They were hiding from God's manifest presence, and they knew it.

Like Adam and Eve, we all reach for our masks, our impersonations, our flimsy fig-leaf cover-ups when we are out of step with God. In fact, we are very good at disguising the fact that we have failed miserably. Our nature is so twisted that we would do just about anything to avoid a face-to-face confrontation with the tangible presence of God. We have an emotional and spiritual warehouse the size of the Smithsonian Institute filled to the brim with cover-ups. In one way or another, every costume hidden in the warehouse has the exact same purpose: to keep us from facing the manifest presence of God.

Cover-ups and Idols

In our culture, a cover-up is what women modestly wear on their way to the beach or pool in order to avoid overexposing their bodies. But what is virtuous for women on their way to the beach is not admirable at all for us. Whether at work or worship, cover-ups spell trouble. Unfortunately, hypocrisy, pretense and deception are our second nature. "The heart is deceitful," the Bible says, "above all things" (Jer. 17:9). Modern history is full of business, marital and political cover-ups, including Watergate, Enron and a junkyard full of other tragedies. Virtually every financial scandal or act of marital infidelity involves a cover-up somewhere, and each refers back to that first cover-up in the Garden of Eden. It is one thing to want to disguise our motives from people; it is another to want to disguise ourselves from God.

Another name for a cover-up is an *idol*. An idol is anything that replaces or displaces the manifest presence of God. Allow me to illustrate.

When Moses was up on the flaming mountain staring eyeball to eyeball with God's manifest presence, the people down in the valley were agitated (see Exod. 19, 32). The Israelites saw the fire of God's presence covering the mountain, and it made them terribly uncomfortable. They didn't like God invading their space. With the heat of God's presence breathing down their necks, the people whom God had just brought out of Egypt built for themselves an idol.

A cover-up.

God on fire has an overarching enemy—an enemy we might not suspect. We are not talking about the blatant street sins of illicit sex and narcotics or the false religions of Islam, Hinduism or Buddhism. No, it is far more subtle, far more insidious and far more unsuspecting. The real enemy of the fire of God's manifest presence is lukewarm Christianity. The force behind lukewarm Christianity is a legion of demons some people refer to as "religious spirits." These religious spirits are knockoffs. Counterfeits. From the garden until now, they have masqueraded as helpers, as assets to genuine believers. Their goal is to prevent people from seeking the one true God and to settle for the outward and superficial. They consume followers of Christ with outward religious rituals that prevent them from developing a personal relationship with the true

God through Jesus Christ. If these spirits are unsuccessful in preventing us from developing a personal relationship with God, they will implement their final strategy: to keep us from living in the fire of God's manifest presence. Any religious experience that does not lead us to an encounter with the fire of God's manifest presence is a big ripoff. A fruitless vine. A rainless cloud. An idol. It promises great things and yet leaves us empty.

Idols come in various shapes and sizes. There are idols of religion, idols of sexual brokenness, idols of generational issues and idols of mental and emotional dysfunction. In one way or another, all idols are erected to fill a void caused by the absence of God's manifest presence. Even Christians who lack the flaming manifest presence of God will intuitively reach for idols. Sure, we would rarely say consciously, "What can I do to fill the void of the fire of God's manifest presence? Oh, I know! Let me build an idol." We are far too sophisticated for that! Instead we have invented a religious cover-up, a more subtle idolatry.

I want to let you in on a secret. I'm intimately acquainted with these specific kinds of idols, because I have erected all of them. Unintentionally, of course, but I am guilty nonetheless. And yet God has been faithful to call me out on my idolatry. He's exposed my idols and enabled me to dismantle them. When you read the following list, you will discover a bunch of what we might call good things gone bad. See if you can identify with these.

Religious idol Number 1: religious activity. As a young Christian, I was involved in Bible studies, youth activities, outreach opportunities and anything else I could do in small groups with my Christian friends. My treadmill of activity made me feel better about myself. I thought that God must be impressed with my zeal. My work *for* God took the place of my relationship *with* God. It was, therefore, an idol.

Religious idol Number 2: Bible doctrine. I would read the Bible, striving for more knowledge. I enjoyed debating Bible issues with both Christian and non-Christian friends. It became a source of pride for me to be able to prove my point. My knowing *about* God took the place of *knowing* God. It was, therefore, an idol.

Religious idol Number 3: Christian fellowship. I was out every night of the week with my friends. I excused it because they were Christian friends. However, the truth was that I didn't want to be alone—not even alone with God. Looking back on that season in my life, I realize now that my addiction to Christian fellowship was not leading me to encounter God but keeping me from it. It was, therefore, an idol.

Religious idol Number 4: morality and ethics. In my high school I was one of a few virgins—and I was proud of it! Even at a Christian college, my morality, while certainly not unique, was still a distinguishing characteristic in which I prided myself. The problem was, I was unconsciously hiding from God behind my own morality. It was, therefore, an idol.

After examining this list, you might be wondering, *What's the problem with these things?* I don't blame you. On the surface these are all noble works. Obviously, I have not gotten rid of all these activities or disciplines. No, I got rid of the idols. Rather than hiding behind these activities or treating any of them as an end, they became a means to the higher calling of encountering Christ. Demolishing these idols was a lengthy process. It involved exposing my superficiality, my twisted motivation and, worst, my pride. All idols are a source of pride. That's why they are so subtle and so painful to remove. When we encounter the manifest presence of God, on the other hand, we are exposed. Our pride is dragged out into the open, and for the first time we are free to be ourselves and to come out from hiding.

Jesus, the Idol Buster

During His earthly ministry, Jesus loved everyone. He made friends with some unlikely people, including prostitutes, tax collectors and sinners. However, the one group of people with whom He often took issue all had one thing in common: hypocrisy. The Pharisees and Sadducees were devout and disciplined in the areas of religious activity, biblical doctrine and morality. Hmm, they sound a lot like me.

None of these activities was inherently evil. They were actually all good things that were intended to be a means by which the religious leaders could encounter God's manifest presence. The activities *became* evil the moment they became an end in themselves, and subsequently, a substitute for God's manifest presence. Remember: an idol is anything that usurps the place of God's tangible presence.

Confronting these religious leaders' habit of settling for doctrine or Bible knowledge as an idol, Jesus said, "You diligently study the Scriptures because you think that by them you possess eternal life. These are the Scriptures that testify about me" (John 5:39). Rather than downplaying the role of scripture, He repositioned it as a means to a higher end: to better know Him. As C.S. Lewis said, "A man can't be always defending the truth; there must be a time to feed on it."[45] When we properly feed on the Bible, we encounter God.

Confronting their treadmill of religious activity that was obviously a pretense, Jesus also said, "These people honor me with their lips, but their hearts are far from me" (Mark 7:6).

Also confronting their use of morality and ethics as a superficial substitute, Jesus cried, "You clean the outside of the cup and dish, but inside they are full of greed and self-indulgence. . . . You are like whitewashed tombs, which look beautiful on the outside but on the inside are full of dead men's bones and everything unclean" (Matt. 23:25, 27).

Finally, confronting their infatuation with their own reputation, Jesus stated, "They love to pray standing in the synagogues and on the street corners to be seen by men" (Matt. 6:5).

Jesus did not want these religious people to settle for proximity rather than His presence. Performance, activity, knowledge and morality all have the potential to become cover-ups or idols that give us a false sense of security.

In contrast, each of these disciplines—service, Bible reading, fellowship and morality—is intended to lead people to encounter God's manifest presence. Unfortunately, then as now, they can also barricade us from God's presence. God wants us to utilize each of these disciplines, as well as others, as a means by which we encounter Him.

Turn Around

When the apostle John heard the trumpet blast, something awakened inside his soul. It shook him to the core. Yes, he'd previously known Jesus, but his knowledge of Jesus was like preschool learning compared to the graduate study he was about to enter.

It started with the trumpet blast, because God always initiates. He goes first, and we follow. Always. The trumpet blast was behind John, because he, like the rest of humankind, was pointing in the wrong direction—with his back toward God's presence.

"I turned around," John recorded, "to see the voice that was speaking to me" (Rev. 1:12). The call to turn around is the call to repent. It is a voluntary choice to take off the cover-ups. It is the call to remove the masks, fig leaves or whatever we've stitched together in our efforts to hide and to avoid the manifest presence of God. When God extended to John this come-and-get-it invitation to His manifest presence, He was looking for an affirmative answer.

Just as God called John to turn around in order to encounter the manifest presence of God, He is also calling each of us to turn around and repent in order to do the same. It is no surprise that John later calls the seven churches to repent. In a string of only fifty sentences, he uses the word "repent" seven times (see Rev. 2:5, 16, 21, 22; 3:3, 19).

God is speaking similarly to us. He is saying, "Repent. Remove your fig leaves, your cover-ups, your religious activity and whatever else you hide behind. I want you to turn around and return to your relationship with Me."

I Turned Around

The miracle of Christ is that we who turned our backs on God, we who grabbed our cover-ups and tried our level best to run and hide, have now been found. His great search and rescue has not only located us but has realigned our hearts and reoriented our dispositions. Through Christ God has removed our hearts of granite and replaced them with tender, responsive hearts of flesh (see Ezek. 11:19). He has replaced our wish to flee from His presence with the compelling motivation to seek His face. We who were once bone tired under the yoke of religious obligation are now capable of becoming tireless marathon runners, gaining more bounce in our stride with every mile.

Let's quickly admit there is nothing more intimidating than the prospect of our humanity facing the tangible presence of God. Like fire, God's manifest presence instantly burns up our fig leaves. He incinerates our idols. Our deception, cover-ups, masks and charades are cremated in a few nanoseconds. Our immediate impulse to such exposure is to recoil and think, *Oh no! There is nowhere to hide. The all-seeing God has just scanned my inner life like an MRI does. I feel exposed and ashamed. Naked and vulnerable.*

But here's the truth: this all-knowing God who consumes our cover-ups in the fire of His presence is also our all-loving God, the Redeemer. He has invited us into a deep, open-face, just-as-I-am, nothing-to-hide relationship with Him. Our *Oh no! There is nowhere to hide* quickly becomes *Oh good! I don't have to hide.*

There is only one reality that can help us make this kind transition in our hearts and minds: the fire of God's manifest presence. It is only when we see the light of the knowledge of the glory of God shining in the face of Jesus Christ that we can truly be ourselves. No more masks, no more cover-ups and no more hypocrisy needed.

Jesus not only called His friend John to turn around, He calls you and me to turn around as well. When we turn, we discover the truth of what Tozer said: "Throughout the history of humanity, there have been many great discoveries. I'm not sure which one we could point to and say, 'That's the greatest discovery in the world,' but for the hungry heart, there is but one discovery that satisfies it: the discovery of the manifest, conspicuous presence of God."[46]

God on Fire in History

Imagine fifty thousand business people gathering in prayer groups every day on their lunch break in New York City. It actually happened! It was a genuine move of the Holy Spirit known as the Layman's Prayer Revival, and it lasted for over two years, between 1857 and 1859.

Jeremiah Lanphier was a forty-year-old business person who distributed Bibles and Christian tracts with what he felt was very little impact, until he felt prompted by God to pray and to invite others to join him. "Going my rounds in the performance of my duty one day," Lanphier writes, "the idea was suggested to my mind that an hour of prayer, from twelve to one o'clock would be beneficial to businessmen, who usually in great numbers take the hour for rest and refreshment. The idea was to have singing, prayer, exhortation, relation of religious experience, and as the case might be, that none should be required to stay the whole hour."[47]

On September 23, 1857, Lanphier knelt alone for the first thirty minutes in the upper lecture room of Old North Dutch Reformed Church in New York City. He wanted an outpouring of the Holy Spirit, and God had something in mind that exceeded his wildest imaginations.[48] By the end of the first hour, six others were praying with him. Their prayers were free and spontaneous, much unlike the formal routine meetings people were used to attending. On the next Wednesday twenty people gathered with him. On the third Wednesday thirty to forty more gathered to pray together. By October 14 over one hundred people were meeting for prayer, many of them coming under great conviction of sin.

Other churches started similar meetings, and within six months fifty thousand people were meeting daily in New York City. Many churches recorded dramatic and specific answers to prayer, and three thousand were converted, including a number of prominent people. Ten crusades were held in nearby Newark, New Jersey, and ten thousand came to Christ.

The hunger for corporate prayer spread up the East Coast to Vermont, New Hampshire, Connecticut and Massachusetts and out to the Midwest, including the cities of Cincinnati, Cleveland, Louisville, Indianapolis, Detroit, Chicago and St. Louis. At one noon prayer gathering in Kalamazoo, Michigan, a praying wife requested prayers for her unconverted husband. All at once a stout, burly man rose and said, "I am the man.

I have a pious, praying wife, and this request must be for me. I want you to pray for me." As soon as he sat down in the middle of the room that was now full with the sobs and tears of the praying, another man rose and said, "I am that man. I have a praying wife. She prays for me. And now she asks you to pray for me. I am sure I am the man. I want you to pray for me." Five other men made similar statements. The power of God fell on the meeting. Almost five hundred conversions were recorded in that town alone.[49]

At this time there was such a tangible sense of the power of God's presence across the East Coast that it was once described as "a zone of heavenly influence." On one occasion the battleship *North Carolina* was anchored in New York City harbor with more than a thousand crewmen. Four sailors began a prayer meeting on the ship and began to sing. Other sailors were so overwhelmed by the sense of God's manifest presence that they began crying for mercy. Night after night, so many hardened sailors were brought to repentance that they had to notify other coastal cities to send ministers to come and pray with the repentant crewman.[50]

Chapter Takeaways

- Humanity has collectively been pointing in the wrong direction.
- An idol is anything that replaces the manifest presence of God.
- My *Oh no! There is nowhere to hide* quickly becomes, *Oh good! I don't have to hide.*

Back to our friend, John the apostle. On the command of Christ, he turned around and was incinerated. *Ruined.* Like I had in high school, John had met his match. Let's discover exactly what it means to be ruined by the manifest presence of Christ.

Ruined in the Fire

About three in the morning, as we were continuing instant in prayer, the power of God came mightily upon us, insomuch that many cried out for exceeding joy and many fell to the ground. As soon as we recovered a little from that awe and amazement at the presence of His majesty, we broke out with one voice, "We praise Thee, O God; we acknowledge Thee to be the Lord."[51]
John Wesley

When I saw him, I fell at his feet as though dead.
Revelation 1:17

RUINED. Wasted. Left for dead. When John took one look at the exalted Christ, his soul was instantly incinerated. It was like he was reduced to a pile of ashes. Instantaneously falling flat on the ground with his face in the dust, his body responded with an almost involuntary reflex to a single glimpse of the risen Christ. There is only one force on earth that slams the human soul with such impact: the manifest presence of God.

When was the last time your soul was reduced to a pile of ashes in the presence of God?

At His Feet

John took one look at the glorified Christ, and he was like burnt toast. He wrote, "When I saw him, I fell at his feet as though dead." This is a raw and honest description of what happens when humanity has a head-on collision with God. There is the outward response: "I fell at his feet." There is the inward response: "as though dead." What makes these responses even more unexpected is that the apostle John knew Jesus very well.

In fact, the argument can be made that no one knew Jesus better than John. He was often included with Jesus in His inner circle of friends along with Peter and James (see Luke 9:28). He was the only disciple who was close and familiar enough to lay his head on Jesus' shoulder (see John 13:23–25). John was also the only disciple to be given the assignment by Jesus from the cross to care for Jesus' mother, Mary (see John 19:27). He is the only follower of Christ referred to as the beloved disciple (see John 13:23).

Suddenly this Navy Seal follower of Christ, who stood head and shoulders above even his fellow disciples in terms of intimacy with Jesus, found himself flat on his face. It is one thing for soldiers to hit the dirt when trying to avoid enemy fire or for a hunter to crawl on all fours when sneaking up on his prey, but this was different. This falling face down had nothing to do with self-preservation or with any effort to gain a positional advantage. Quite the contrary! It was more a response to having self annihilated; one in which John was the hunted, not the hunter.

Falling facedown before God is nothing new. Both modern and biblical history have on record many fall-on-your-face, or at least fall-on-your knees, in worship moments as people have encountered God's manifest presence:

- Abraham fell flat on his face. (see Gen. 17:3)
- Moses fell flat on his face. (see Deut. 9:18)
- Joshua fell flat on his face. (see Josh. 5:14)
- All of Israel fell flat on their faces. (see 2 Chron. 7:3)

- King Jehoshaphat fell flat on his face. (see 2 Chron. 20:18)
- Peter fell on his knees. (see Luke 5:8)

One of the many world-class, fall-on-your-face-in-worship encounters took place three-and-a-half thousand years ago. A group of Hebrew worshipers gathered around the Tent of Meeting, and God showed up. The Tent was constructed with the express purpose of being the location where God's manifest presence would dwell. This particular account in Leviticus 9:23–24 vividly describes the play-by-play sequence of events: "Moses and Aaron then went into the Tent of Meeting. When they came out, they blessed the people; and the glory of the Lord appeared to all the people. Fire came out from the presence of the Lord and consumed the burnt offering and the fat portions on the altar. And when all the people saw it, they shouted for joy and fell facedown."

Another world-class, fall-on-your-face worship encounter took place on Mount Carmel when Elijah prayed down fire. When the fire of God's presence came, the people fell facedown and cried in loud voices, "The Lord—he is God! The Lord—he is God!" (1 Kings 18:39).

Yet another world-class moment took place at the completion of the temple. When Solomon finished praying, the fire of God's manifest presence came down from heaven and incinerated his offering. The glory of God's tangible presence was so thick in the temple that the priests were immobilized, as if they had been hit by a stun-gun. "When all the Israelites saw the fire coming down and the glory of the Lord above the temple, they knelt on the pavement with their faces to the ground" (2 Chron. 7:3).

The same pattern continues into the New Testament. When the pre-Christian Paul (named Saul) first encountered the manifest presence of God on the dirt road to Damascus, the fire of God's manifest presence flashed in front of him and he immediately "fell to the ground" (Acts 9:4).

Each of these accounts illustrates an irrefutable pattern. When God reveals Himself in the fire of His tangible presence, the automatic response is to fall facedown in worship. There is something perfectly appropriate about falling facedown before God, even for those who know him best, as did the apostle John.

We need more fall-on-your-face-in-worship encounters with God. God has indeed been stalking us even as He stalked Moses and Aaron, Elijah and Solomon, Paul and John. It is God who has the positional advantage, and we are in His cross hairs. When He sovereignly chooses to reveal the all-consuming inferno of His manifest presence, we too will respond like the others who have gone before us. We will fall facedown in surrender, and worship Christ.

As Though Dead

Far more significant than the outward response of falling on his face is John inwardly feeling "as though dead." Something had died. If a paramedic had checked John's vitals, certainly John would have had a heart rate. His blood pressure would have been in range, though perhaps elevated. His brain waves would have been strong. Yet, on some deeper level, John experienced a death. His was a death to self—to self-interest, self-preservation, self-will, self-seeking and self-defense. He experienced what Jesus taught all His followers: "If anyone would come after me, he must deny himself and take up his cross daily and follow me" (Luke 9:23).

The manifest presence of God has a way of cutting through the surface of our lives and exposing the subtleties of our sinful selfishness that often hides in the depths of our souls. Like a skilled surgeon's scalpel, God's Holy Spirit can penetrate our superficial self-understanding and instantly expose caverns of deceitful wickedness hiding in our hearts.

The apostle Paul knew the reality of *God on fire*, and he embraced the reality of death to self. He claimed, "I have been crucified with Christ and I no longer live, but Christ lives in me. The life I live in the body, I live by faith in the Son of God, who loved me and gave himself for me" (Gal. 2:20). Paul died to his own sin (see Rom. 6:2) because he was baptized into Christ's death (see Rom. 6:4) and united with Christ in His resurrected life (see Rom. 6:5).

"I have been crucified" is a radical statement. Few, if any, have ever been crucified and lived to talk about it—with one notable exception.

Dead or Alive

You may be wondering, *I thought we were talking about revival, and now we are talking about death. Which is it? Does the manifest presence of God kill us or make us alive?* The answer is an emphatic *yes!*

Resurrection always follows crucifixion, not the other way around. We are living in a Christian culture that has forgotten this critical sequence. We have forgotten that there must be death before there is reconciliation. Perhaps the only way to restore the sequence is for us to re-encounter the reviving manifest presence of Christ.

When John first encountered the manifest presence of Christ, he fell at His feet as though dead.

When Isaiah first encountered the manifest presence of Christ, he fell at His feet and cried, "Woe to me! . . . I am ruined!" (Isa. 6:5).

When Peter first encountered the manifest presence of God of Christ, he fell down and cried, "Go away from me, Lord; I am a sinful man!" (Luke 5:8).

Even the great English Puritan leader Richard Baxter said, "I preached as a dying man to dying men."[52]

Jonathan Edwards reported this same pattern during the Great Awakening. He writes, "It was then a frequent thing for many to be so extraordinarily seized with terror in hearing the word, by the Spirit of God convincing them of sin, that they fell down, and were carried out of the church, and they afterwards proved more solid and lively Christians."[53]

These who encountered the manifest presence of Christ were humbled into submission. They were exposed, convicted, cleansed and yes, delivered. For perhaps the first time in their lives, they were brought face to face with God and simultaneously with themselves. Their vision of God was spectacular. It was glorious, breathtaking, inspiring, riveting, captivating and yes, life-giving. The vision they had previously had of themselves and of their own glory was crushing in comparison.

Crucifixion is terminal. It is a brutal means of execution. It takes no prisoners and leaves no survivors.

Ruined Forever

The word "ruined" is often reserved to describe food that has perished. Unrefrigerated meat or milk left on the counter is ruined, or spoiled, and needs to be thrown in the trash because it is no longer useful to us. Of all words, this is the one that the prophet Isaiah carefully selected to describe the way he felt after coming face to face with the raging presence of God (see Isa. 6:5). He saw the Lord seated on the throne of the entire universe. In a similar vision to the one our friend John had of Christ, Isaiah saw the Lord high and exalted. His regal robe flowed in the temple. He saw angels crying out, "Holy, holy, holy is the LORD Almighty; the whole earth is full of his glory" (Isa. 6:3). The resounding sound of the angels' voices caused the threshold to shake as the smoke of God's glory billowed like pyrotechnics. All the prophet could say was, "Woe to me! . . . I am ruined [wasted]!" (Isa. 6:5).

Let's break this down.

Woe. This is a word that indicates liability, an indefensible exposure. Woe is a big gulp of it-is-too-late, there-is-no-where-to-hide remorse in the presence of an infinitely superior God.

Woe to me. This phrase shows that there is no finger-pointing, no sharing of the blame. This time it is all on me. I belly up to the bar of God's accountability and assume full responsibility for my actions and attitudes, my thoughts and words.

I cried. This is, rather plainly, sorrow. Grief. Unspeakable pain of regret followed by screams of repentance.

I am ruined. The Hebrew word is *damah*. It is used only sixteen times in the Old Testament and literally means to disintegrate or unravel. It means to come apart at the seams, to be destroyed or to cease to exist.[54] There is only a single charge that can detonate this level of nuclear-meltdown repentance within the human soul: the manifest presence of God. All fig-leaf cover-ups decompose, utterly unraveling in the presence of Almighty God.

A flaming coal. To culminate this *God on fire* encounter for Isaiah, an angel took a live coal from before the altar. Using a set of tongs as if lifting a hot towel, the angel placed the coal on Isaiah's face, touched his lips and announced, "See, this has touched your lips; your guilt is taken away and your sin atoned for" (Isa. 6:7).

As we will discover in the next chapter, death to self does not mean that personal identity is irrelevant or is lost in the process. On the contrary, we are never more alive, more unique, more us than when we learn to live in the flaming reality of the manifest presence of Christ.

What we die to, on the other hand, is everything that distorts, corrupts and disguises our true identity. In Christ, we die to twisted pride, self-hatred, vain conceit, bitter jealousy, sexual brokenness, selfish ambition, destructive lusts and false gods. We die to pretense, deceit, hypocrisy and other counterfeit cover-ups. We die, ultimately, to self-consciousness. Like Adam and Eve who were naked and not ashamed as they walked with God in the cool of the day, in Christ we are able to return to the glorious state of self-forgetfulness.

Just to be clear, the only way to truly be yourself—the person God has made you to be—is to live in the manifest presence of God. Living in the fire is where you become self-forgetful, where you are free to be the *real* you.

Never Settle for Less

Once we taste the manifest presence of God, we are marked for life. From that point forward we know that this is why we are here. We will never again want to settle for anything less. We are ruined. Plain old religious activity—simply reading the Bible as an end in itself or keeping the church machinery moving—will never again for as long as we live satisfy the deepest longings of our soul.

When the apostle Paul recognized all that God had done for him in Christ, he too fell to his knees in prayer. Let's use his words now to God in prayer:

> *For this reason I kneel before the Father, from whom his whole family in heaven and on earth derives its name. I pray that out of his glorious riches he may strengthen you with power through his Spirit in your inner being, so that Christ may dwell in your hearts through faith. And I pray that you, being rooted and established in love, may have power, together with all the saints, to grasp how wide and long and high and deep is the love of Christ, and to know this love that*

surpasses knowledge—that you may be filled to the measure of all the fullness of God. (Eph. 3:14–19)

God on Fire in History

St. Augustine is honored by church historians as the doctor of the church and the theological father of the Reformation. Virtually every philosopher and theologian in the last millennium has been profoundly influenced by Augustine, including Thomas Aquinas, Martin Luther, John Calvin, R.C. Sproul, John Piper and even Jean-Paul Sartre. Augustine is one of the most prolific writers of all time, with over three hundred and fifty preserved sermons and more than one hundred books, including enormous volumes like *City of God*, a compilation of twenty-two distinct books. What is often overlooked is that Augustine was not only a brilliant theologian but a practicing supernaturalist who frequently encountered the manifest presence of God. He wrote extensively on the manifest power of God dramatically demonstrated in physical healings and deliverances from demonic bondage.

Augustine was born November 13, 354, and converted to Christianity at age thirty-three. He was baptized with his son, Adeodatus, on Resurrection Sunday (Easter). A powerful intellectual and a stunning orator, Augustine marshaled his communication firepower to defend authentic Christianity. He worked tirelessly and exercised keen self-discipline by eating sparingly and generously selling many of his possessions, giving the money raised to the poor. He resisted any form of sensual indulgence in order to keep his heart pure before God.

Early in his Christian faith, Augustine wrote *Of True*

Religion, which actually exposed the absence of God's manifest presence in the church.[55] He later wrote *The Retraction*,[56] in which he documented seventy distinct miracles. He indicated that he could "fill several volumes" with the numerous healings and supernatural manifestation that he saw during his life and ministry.[57] Several healings of terminal diseases were recorded. Augustine expressed frustration and disappointment that more public testimony was not being given to the dramatic miracles.

One Resurrection Sunday a young man named Paul and his sister Palladra entered the public place of worship in plain sight of hundreds of fellow seekers. They both suffered from chronic convulsions and seizures. That day Paul suddenly fell prostrate under a convulsion and laid perfectly still as if in a trance. Soon his convulsions stopped, and people were awestruck. As Paul rose to his feet, appearing perfectly normal and praising God, the people in the basilica burst into joyful celebration. Despite the fact that it was Resurrection Sunday, Augustine chose to preach very little in order to allow the church to "meditate in their own minds on the divine eloquence of the divine deed rather than to listen to any mere words of [his]." Three days later, Palladra entered the sanctuary seeking God for healing. When she came to the exact place her brother was touched, she too fell motionless to the floor, only to rise moments later, thoroughly healed. "Such a clamor of wonderment went up," Augustine wrote, "I thought it would never end."[58]

This revealing of God's manifest presence continued until the day Augustine died. As he lay on his death bed, a visitor came seeking healing and claiming that in a dream it had been revealed to him that he would receive his healing if the ailing pastor prayed for him. Augustine laid hands on his guest, inviting God to come and manifest healing. The man left completely well.

Chapter Takeaways

- Ruined. Wasted. One look at the exalted Christ, and we are instantly incinerated.
- History is full of fall-on-your-face-in-worship moments when people encountered God's manifest presence.
- The single charge that reduces the human soul to a pile of ashes is the manifest presence of God.

Our God is a consuming fire. He consumes our idols and our preoccupations. He kills our sin so that He might redeem our dignity and fulfill our destiny. Now let's discover what lies beyond our death to self: the resurrection life of Christ at work in us.

A Hand from the Fire

The Holy Spirit must anoint me for the work, fire me, and so
vividly convince me that such and such a way is mine to aim at,
or I shall not go, I will not, I dare not. . . . Nothing but the fire
of the most Holy Spirit of God can make the offering holy and
unblameable and acceptable in his sight.[59]
Oswald Chambers

Then he placed his right hand on me.
Revelation 1:17

IT is an unmistakable pattern throughout history that anyone
whom God uses to impact our world likely received his or
her calling from an encounter with the manifest presence of
Christ. I'd go as far as to say that the reason so many Christian
workers are dropping out of the ministry today is because their
calling was never the result of such an encounter.

Soon after John fell on his face, he recounts, "Then [Jesus]
placed his right hand on me." John had told us earlier that
Jesus' right hand was holding seven gigantic stars—balls of
flaming gasses. Now he tells us that Jesus placed this same
right hand on his scalp. You can almost feel the heat. Smokin'!

Under normal conditions, death marks an end. The body
goes in the box. The box goes in the ground. The end. For Christ,
however, death is a mere blip on the screen. He can bust up

a funeral like no one else. When He leads us to crucifixion—death to self—it only terminates sin and its power to destroy us. Jesus always follows death with resurrection. Jesus is not into killing people. He is into killing what is out to kill us so that He can make us fully alive.

Imagine feeling the hand of God on your shoulder or your forehead. Many of us will never experience that sensation as John did, but all of us can know the reality of what God's hand transmitted to John. We too can receive the life-transmitting, confidence-building, dignity-restoring, destiny-affirming, purpose-empowering hand of God that lifts us up out of our sin casket and gets us back in the game. We all need our own then-he-placed-his-right-hand-on-me moment.

The right hand of God signifies great honor. In a court of law, those who are about to testify are asked to lift their right hand. When we greet one another, we extend our right hand as a gesture of warm engagement. At least five specific times, the New Testament explicitly identifies the present location of the Son of God as at the right hand of God the Father.[60] Similarly, when Jesus extends His hand toward His faithful servant John, He lifts the hand of highest honor.

God's Body Parts

Jesus has a physical body. He's had one ever since His incarnation in Bethlehem. He will have one for all eternity. God the Father, on the other hand, is Spirit. He is not localized in a physical body, so any reference to His hands, head, feet, face, ears or mouth are figurative, anthropomorphic references (assigning to God human-like characteristics). When the Bible uses these body parts to refer to Father God, they are normally references to His manifest presence, as the omnipresence of God has no hands, ears, fee, mouth or face. For example, when God works in a miraculous way, He is described by His mighty hand and outstretched arm (see Deut. 4:34; 7:19; 11:2; 26:8). Prayers for the arm of the Lord to be revealed (see Isa. 51:9; 53:1) are requests that God manifest His power and might. God is also described as having eyes (see 1 Sam. 3:18; 15:25; 2 Chron. 14:2; 29:6; Amos 9:8), ears (see 2 Kings 19:16; Dan. 9:18; James 5:4), feet (see Exod. 24:10) and a mouth (see 2 Chron. 35:22; 36:12 in NKJV; Matt. 4:4). Each of these word pictures of God's "body parts" are simply attempts to illustrate that our God is more intimately and tangibly involved in our world than we realize.

God's Face

There are few more vivid descriptions of God's manifest presence than those depicting His face. Jacob was the first to encounter God's face in a life-defining moment. After an all-night wrestling match, having his hip socket permanently disjointed and undergoing a permanent identity change, he said, "I saw God face to face" (Gen. 32:30). He named the spot where it happened Peniel, meaning "face of God." Later in the Old Testament, we learn that King David cried out "Do not hide your face from me" (Ps. 27:9), and again, "Make your face shine upon us" (Ps. 80:7, 19). Even Daniel ached to see God's face (see Dan. 9:17).

When the priests were given explicit instructions regarding how they were to bless the people, there was a strong reference to the face of God: "The Lord bless you and keep you; the Lord make his face shine upon you and be gracious to you; the Lord turn his face toward you and give you peace" (Num. 6:24–26).

Let's hit pause. Reread those verses. If you don't mind writing in your book, circle the word "face." It is almost shocking to think about the power and influence of these words. God gave the priests the authority to verbally call forth and impart the manifest presence of God to the people. This is an interesting case study, for sure. If the priests of Moses were assigned the role of verbally communicating the manifest presence of Christ, how much more should it be the norm for us on this side of His resurrection.

Similar to the priestly blessing, the psalmist cried out for God's manifest presence: "May God be gracious to us and bless us and make his face shine upon us" (Ps. 67:1). Crying out for the manifest presence of God's face should be part of the normal daily prayer life of every healthy believer. For all of us who previously hid from the face of God, our conversion into Face-seekers is truly one of God's great miracles.

When the apostle Paul defined the distinction between the Old Covenant and the New Covenant, he acknowledged that both covenants contain the glory of God's manifest presence as well as illustrate a number of benefits, although the New Covenant reveals significantly more than does the Old Covenant.

Old Covenant	New Covenant
Written on stone	Written on human hearts (2 Cor. 3:3)
Letter of law that kills	Letters of Holy Spirit that give life (2 Cor. 3:6)
Fading glory	Surpassing, ever-increasing glory (2 Cor. 3:7, 18)
Limited power	All-surpassing power (2 Cor. 4:7)

The trump card of the New Covenant is the that same God who said "Let there be light" at the beginning of creation has now "made his light shine in our hearts to give us the light of the knowledge of the glory of God in the face of Christ" (2 Cor. 4:6). This ongoing, perpetual access to see the face of Christ is the promise of perpetual access into God's manifest presence.

God's Hand

When the enthroned Christ extended His hand and placed it on top of the paralyzed John, it brought healing. It affirmed and empowered John. Keep in mind: this is the same hand that healed leprous skin, blind eyes and paraplegic bodies. It is the same hand that formed our physical bodies (see Ps. 119:73) and knit us together in our mother's wombs (see Ps. 139:13–14). It is the same hand that created the heavens, including the stars, planets and all the solar systems (see Isa. 48:13). It is the same hand that the prophets frequently referred to when they encountered God's manifest presence (see Ezek. 1:3; 3:14, 22; 8:1, 3; 33:22; 37:1; 40:1; Dan. 5:23; Amos 1:8). In fact, Nehemiah attributed to his success the fact that the hand of God was with him (see Neh. 2:8, 18). He and his contemporaries knew that when the invisible God sovereignly chooses to conspicuously invade our space, it is the hand of God.

John was face down "as though dead" until he felt the hand. The right hand, the hand of highest honor, was extended to John, and the apostle instantly knew that there was life after death. Though utterly overwhelmed and overshadowed by the splendor of Christ, he was affirmed. Validated. Even though he trembled in God's presence and lay prostrate in the dirt, feeling totally unworthy, the right hand called him back into service.

Placing His hand squarely on the apostle's shoulder, our Lord Jesus gave John his new assignment: "Write, therefore, what you have seen" (Rev. 1:19). The same Christ who initially said to John by the banks of the Sea of Galilee, "Follow me and I will make you fishers of men," is now re-commissioning John on the coastline of Patmos: "Write what you see." As I mentioned earlier, the call of God on an individual's life is always the result of an encounter with the manifest presence of Christ. Always.

The proof is right there in the Bible.

Abraham left his idols in Ur for one reason: he encountered the manifest presence of God. Jacob underwent an identity change and walked with a limp for the rest of his life for one reason: he encountered the manifest presence of God. Moses left his self-imposed hiatus on the back side of the desert for one reason: he encountered the manifest presence of God. David left his sheep in order to fulfill his higher calling for one reason: he encountered the manifest presence of God. Saul stopped persecuting Christians and embraced his new identity as the apostle Paul for one reason: he encountered the manifest presence of God. Finally, our friend John was no longer a sidelined apostle and a religious prisoner of Rome on the isolated island of Patmos. He took on his new assignment of writing the final book in the Bible for one reason. You got it! He encountered the manifest presence of God.

We have seen this same pattern throughout church history, from Zinzendorf to Augustine, Wesley to Whitefield, Evan Roberts to Jeremiah Lanphier. Each of these mighty leaders was called and commissioned only *after* he encountered the manifest presence of God in Christ. It should not be surprising to us that so many pastors today are dropping out of the ministry and just as many missionaries are returning home from their overseas assignments. Too many in our generation have lost sight of God's manifest presence. What keeps a pastor in the pulpit and a missionary in the trenches is the deep-down conviction that he is called of God. Such a call cannot be fabricated. No amount of motivational seminars, self-help books or therapy sessions will talk anyone into sticking with this stuff when the going gets tough. Bible reading, prayer, support groups, fasting and worship CDs are all great but will not solely convince anyone to hold the course either. What is needed is a fresh encounter with God. We need a He-placed-

His-right-hand-on-me, white-hot encounter with God.

How would you like for Christ to place His hand on your head the way He placed it on John's? God extends His hand to each of us. The Bible invites us into a hands-on relationship with God by saying, "Humble yourselves, therefore, under God's mighty hand, that he may lift you up in due time" (1 Pet. 5:6). While it is unrealistic to expect to feel the physical hand of Christ on our forehead, God wants to impart to us all that His hand represents. "He placed his right hand on me" was in many ways the defining moment in the book of the Revelation. Christ's right hand blessed John. It accepted, validated, delivered and empowered him. He was then free to be the man God had designed him to be and to enter into his own destiny. As Henri Nouwen said, "I am deeply convinced that the leader of the future is called to be completely irrelevant and to stand in the world with nothing to offer but his or her own vulnerable self."[61]

Holy, Holy, Holy Hand

Our culture has marginalized holiness. We have become increasingly ambivalent, profane even. God, on the other hand, not only loves holiness, He is holy. You don't hold up the measuring stick of holiness next to God to determine whether or not He qualifies. He is the measuring stick! The only virtue of God—and there are many—that is repeated throughout the Bible in triplicate is that of his holiness. The angels declare nonstop in God's presence, "Holy, holy, holy." The prophet Isaiah heard this declaration, as did John (see Isa. 6:3; Rev. 4:8). Yet we hardly know what it means. Without the manifest presence of Christ, we have no point of reference by which to judge the holy from the unholy.

The Hebrew word for "to be holy" is *quadash*, derived from the root word *qad*, which means to cut or separate. The

New Testament Greek word *hagios* conveys the same idea. Therefore, to be holy means to be separated from the common or the ordinary and to now belong to God. In this sense, the opposite of being holy is not being sinful; it is to be common. Ordinary. Secular.

Clark Williams in his book *The Descent of the Dove* reflects on the true meaning of holiness. He writes, "Piety is not a long struggle against that which is impure or forbidden, rather it is a singleness of heart."[62]

There is, however, another word that bears a strange resemblance to the word "holy" that most people can readily understand—it's the word "mine." When God uses the word "holy," He is essentially saying, "Mine! You now belong to Me." One of the first words a child learns to say soon after "Mama," even at times before "Papa," is "mine." Another child in daycare tries to take her blocks? "Mine!" the child demands. It is planted deep in our DNA to protect our turf and demand our rights. This is what makes encountering the holy-holy-holy presence of God so revolutionizing. The moment our humanity encounters Him, we have a head-on collision with ownership. We who have spent a lifetime demanding "Mine!" come face to face with God who now says "Mine."

When God revealed Himself to Isaiah and the words "Holy, holy, holy" rang in the prophet's ears, Isaiah would never again be the same, because God was saying to him, "Mine! You are now all Mine."

When John saw the exalted Christ and the Lord placed His hand on his shoulder, Jesus was saying, "Mine! You are now all Mine."

When God reveals His manifest presence to His people, He is setting them apart. There is no higher calling. It's a matter of ownership; God's sovereignty in our lives and in our destiny. Will we fight to maintain self-ownership, or will we relinquish ownership of our lives to Christ? There is only one way for any of us to ultimately rediscover holiness and that is to have a fresh encounter with the holiness of God, with His manifest presence. When God places His hand on you and says "Mine!" you will know it. If something in your heart says Yes! I want to declare myself holy to God!" I encourage you to genuinely pray this prayer:

> *Father God, I am bought with a price—the blood of Christ.*[63]
> *I am not my own any longer. I relinquish control to You over my body, my mind, my family, my relationships, my habits, my cares, my resources and my past, present and future. I present my life wholly to God in the name of the Father, Son and Holy Spirit. Stamp "Holy to the Lord" on every cell of my body and in every area of my life.*

God on Fire in History

As a young man, Jonathan Edwards, widely considered one of America's greatest theologians, acknowledged God's ownership over His life and declared himself holy to God. As a teenager he wrote thirty-eight resolutions that would guide his life. By age twenty he had added several more to bring the total to seventy. These guiding statements of resolve began with these words: "Being sensible that I am unable to do anything without God's help, I do humbly entreat him, by his grace, to enable me to keep these resolutions, so far as they are agreeable to his will, for Christ's sake." His resolutions include the following:

- Resolved, never to lose one moment of time, but to

improve it in the most profitable way I possibly can.
- Resolved, to live with all my might, while I do live.
- Resolved, never to do anything which I should be afraid to do if it were the last hour of my life."

Not surprisingly, he added to his list, "Remember to read over these resolutions once a week."[64]

Edwards entered Yale College at the age of twelve and graduated as valedictorian at the head of his class before becoming the third president of Princeton. Describing his own encounter with God, he wrote, "The sense I had of divine things would often of a sudden kindle up, as it were, a sweet burning in my heart. I had a view that for me was extraordinary of the glory of the Son of God as Mediator between God and man, and His wonderful great, full, pure and sweet grace and love, and meek and gentle condescension."[65]

Edwards not only encountered the manifest presence of God, he had a front row seat in one of the world-class, God-encountering movements of all modern history known as America's Great Awakening. He captures his thoughts about the revival in his *Treatise on Religious Affections* as well in his *An Humble Attempt*,[66] perhaps the clearest defense of encountering God's manifest presence ever written:

Extraordinary news of divine things, and the religious affections, were frequently attended with very grave effects on the body. Nature often sunk under the weight of divine discoveries and the strength of the body was taken away. The person was deprived of all abilities to stand or speak. Sometimes the hands were clenched, and the flesh cold, but the senses remaining. The soul at the same time was so strongly drawn toward God and Christ in heaven, that it seemed to the persons as the soul and body would, as it were of themselves, of necessity mount up, leave the earth, and ascend thither.[67]

Edwards frequently used the phrase "abundant effusions of the Holy Spirit"[68] to refer to God's manifest presence.

[God] would appear in his glory, and manifest his compassion to the world of mankind and by an abundance effusion of his Holy Spirit on all the churches. . . . It implies that God himself is the great good desired and sought after; but the blessings pursued are God's gracious presence, the Blessed manifestation of . . . and communication of himself by his Holy Spirit.[69]

"The town seemed to be full of the presence of God," Edwards wrote to summarize the impact of God's manifest presence on his own town of Northampton, Massachusetts.[70]

I know of no one young person in the town who has returned to former ways of looseness and extravagance in any respect, but we still remain a reformed people, and God has evidently made us a new people. For here in this corner of the world, God dwells and manifests his glory.[71]

It was then a frequent thing for many to be so extraordinarily seized with terror in hearing the word, by the Spirit of God convincing them of sin, that they fell down, and were carried out of the church, and they afterwards proved more solid and lively Christians.[72]

Jonathan Edwards lived with a heightened sense of destiny, always pursuing excellence, seeking to maximize every opportunity to the glory of God. He lived with the prayer, "Lord, stamp eternity on my eyeballs."

Chapter Takeaways

- Anyone whom God uses to impact our world likely receives his or her calling from an encounter with the manifest presence of Christ.

- We all need our own then-He-placed-his-right-hand-on-me moment.
- There are few more vivid descriptions of God's manifest presence than those that depict His face.
- When God says, "Holy," He is essentially saying, "Mine! You now belong to Me."

The manifest presence of Christ, as good as it sounds, will remain only a theory for even the clearest thinking Christian until the Holy Spirit turns on the light bulb. Let's discover firsthand, as John did, the vital role the Holy Spirit plays in revealing Christ to us in tangible ways that we can understand.

Holy Spirit on Fire

The power given is not a gift from the Holy Ghost.
He, Himself, is the power.[73]
Hudson Taylor

On the Lord's Day I was in the Spirit.
Revelation 1:10

IF you want to see the Eifel Tower, you need to be in Paris. If you want to see the Western Wall, you need to be in Jerusalem. If you want to see the pyramids, you need to be in Egypt. If you want to see the Great Barrier Reef, you need to be in Australia. And if you want to see the manifest presence of Christ, you need to be in the Spirit.

When the apostle John said "I was in the Spirit," he was not being mystical, peculiar or weird. He was simply under the influence of the Holy Spirit. It was no coincidence that such a significant encounter with the manifest presence of Christ would follow. Whenever God chooses to manifest His presence, the Holy Spirit is always in the vicinity. Always.

"I was in the Spirit" was John's way of saying, "I knew that God was up to something." This kind of occurrence was familiar to him. On the day of Pentecost, when the flaming reality of the Holy Spirit had filled every believer in the upper room, John had learned firsthand what it meant to be "in the Spirit."

It is obvious that being *in the Spirit* is different than the Spirit being in us. John had already been indwelt by the Holy Spirit, but now something categorically different was happening to him. The same Spirit who continually lived within him was manifesting His presence in a tangible and readily recognizable way. Let's take a closer look.

Indwelling Presence

We have already clarified the all-important difference between the omnipresence and the manifest presence of God. We now want to make a further distinction, one between the indwelling presence and the manifest presence. The apostle Paul reminded first-century Christians of God's indwelling presence by asking, "Do you not know that your body is a temple of the Holy Spirit?" (1 Cor. 6:19). Just as the temple was the dwelling place of God in the Old Testament, so the human body is the dwelling place of God for all true followers of Christ. As the temple in Jerusalem had been the localized venue in which God's presence dwelt, the human body has now replaced the temple and is the new venue. The place has changed, but not the presence.

Jewish believers knew that while God's omnipresence lived everywhere, His particular presence lived in the temple. They further knew that because God's Spirit lived in the temple, He could at any moment manifest His presence, demonstrating the relationship between the indwelling presence and the manifest presence of God. Here are a few examples of what this looked like:

- The lamp in the temple was never allowed to extinguish, representing the flame of God's manifest, tangible presence. (see Exod. 25:31–40)
- Priests were assigned shifts to simply watch for the

presence of God to show up. (see Exod. 29, 40)

- Once a year, the high priest entered the Holy of Holies on the Day of Atonement to offer sacrifices for his own sins and for the sins of the nation. When he entered a cord was tied around his ankle as a means of dragging him out, just in case he died while he was in God's presence. (see Exod. 30:10; Lev. 23:27; Num. 25:13)

What set apart the Jewish temple from the Jewish bakery or the Jewish deli were both the indwelling presence and the manifest presence of God. Because God lived in a particular way inside the temple, the people knew that He was likely to also manifest His presence inside the temple. The Jews were aware of the distinction between the indwelling presence and the manifest presence, yet they also knew the close relationship between the two. Because of their confidence in the indwelling presence, they were always looking for the manifest presence. They knew that what set them apart from the other nations on earth was the fact that God was with them—not in theory but in reality.

The Bible teaches that every believer reborn in the Spirit has the indwelling presence of the Holy Spirit. We should, therefore, expect His manifest presence. The first insures the second. However, it is helpful to discern the difference between the two:

Indwelling Presence	Manifest Presence
Biblical	Biblical
Real	Real
True to God's nature	True to God's nature
Means God is inside my life	Means God is tangibly perceived
Exclusively for God's people	Normally for God's people
Not necessarily obvious	Always obvious

The Truthful Spirit

Jesus referred to the Holy Spirit as the Spirit of truth who leads us into all truth. Oswald Chambers, in his classic daily devotional book *My Utmost for His Highest*, identifies the collateral damage of self-deception that occurs when God's Spirit is not active in our lives. He writes, "The deadliest Phariseeism today is not hypocrisy but unconscious unreality."[74]

In her book *Listening Prayer*, Leanne Payne points us in the right direction: "We can all too easily substitute practicing the presence of the self rather than practicing the presence of God. We all too easily practice the self-deceived art of self projection, putting words in God's mouth rather than the other way around. We become both the initiator and the responder, and we become self-deceived in the process."[75] She continues, "People trapped in their own subjectivity are difficult to be around for any length of time."[76] Payne identifies the heart of the problem when she states, "Failure to dwell in the presence of God is the essence of sin—the primary result of the fall. As a result of the fall, humanity slipped from genuine God consciousness into self-consciousness."[77]

The Spirit of truth, on the other hand, is the ultimate reality check. We need the Holy Spirit in order to give us proper perspective not only on ourselves but on Christ.

The Revealing Spirit

The presence of God is like a one-way mirror that has God on one side and us on the other. God can see us, but we can't see Him. At least we can't see Him until He chooses to turn on the light on His side of the mirror. The Holy Spirit is the light, and though present with us all the time, He is invisible. However, when the Holy Spirit chooses to make Himself known to us, everything immediately changes. Bible teacher F.B. Meyers says, "He is like a shaft of light that falls on the Beloved Face, so that as in a photograph, you do not think about the light, nor the origin of the light, but you think about the face that it reveals."[78]

Jesus explained to His disciples the role of the Holy Spirit: "He will testify about me" (John 15:26). He said, "He will bring glory to me by taking from what is mine and making it known to you" (John 16:14). These statements are far-reaching. The Holy Spirit takes everything that Jesus has for us and makes it available. Everything. Paul knew that the Holy Spirit is a revelatory Spirit. He prayed very specifically, "I keep asking that the God of our Lord Jesus Christ, the glorious Father, may give you the Spirit of wisdom and revelation, so that you may know him better" (Eph. 1:17).

Eternal life comes from Christ, but it is quickened, activated and revealed to us by the Holy Spirit: "The Spirit himself testifies with our spirit that we are God's children" (Rom. 8:16).

Victory over stubborn, sinful habits comes from Christ, but it is imparted to us by the Holy Spirit: "If by the Spirit you put to death the misdeeds of the body, you will live" (Rom. 8:13).

The one God who is three Persons dynamically operates in perfect unity. While it is dangerous for us to try too hard to dissect the roles of the Godhead, there are some things we can safely say about the three Persons:

The Father is always sending the Son.
The Son is always being sent by the Father.
The Holy Spirit is always activating the Son.

There are several key moments in which the Bible illustrates the three Persons distinctly and explicitly operating together. During the creation, the one God in three Persons created all things. On all six days of creation, we see that God the Father spoke the Word, the Son went out as the Word, and the Holy Spirit activated the Word (see Gen. 1:2).

During the incarnation the triune God was fully involved. God the Father sent the Son. The Son was sent, and the Holy Spirit activated the virgin ovum of Mary to impregnate her (see Luke 1:35).

During Jesus' baptism the triune God worked in perfect synergy. God the Father spoke, the Son heard the Father's voice, and the Holy Spirit came on Jesus to activate and empower him (see Matt. 3:16–17; Luke 4:17–19).

During the process of a person coming to salvation, the triune God is at work. A single Bible verse succinctly states, "For through him [Jesus] we both have access to the Father by one Spirit" (Eph. 2:18).

It is not surprising that the followers of Christ are to be baptized in the singular name of one triune God: the Father, Son and Holy Spirit (see Matt. 28:19).

You might be wondering, "What does this little discussion on the tri-unity of God have to do with our understanding of God's manifest presence?"

As we have seen, the three Persons of the one true God act together in synergy and cooperation. While their roles may be somewhat distinct, the Persons of the Godhead are always interfacing and collaborating in perfect harmony, and the Holy Spirit is always the activator. When God created the worlds, each Person of the Godhead worked together, and the Holy Spirit activated the word. When the Father sent the Son into the world, each Person worked together, and the Holy Spirit activated the virgin womb. When Jesus was baptized, the triune God was present, and the Holy Spirit empowered Him. Whenever God chooses to manifest His presence to us, the triune God works in perfect harmony, and the Holy Spirit empowers us. The one true, living God is self-revealing, and

He works in unity to reveal His glory and to lead His people to His manifest presence. Here's the bottom line: while the revelation and the encounter are fully the work of the one triune God, His presence is primarily manifested to us by the Holy Spirit.

The Person of the Holy Spirit

It is easy for most believers to comprehend the power of the Holy Spirit. It is not as easy to understand the Personhood of the Holy Spirit. We understand that God the Father is a Person and that God the Son is a Person because we can relate to the image of a father and his son from our human relationships. It is not quite as easy for us to recognize the personhood of the Holy Spirit. The word pictures used in the Bible to refer to the Holy Spirit do not make it any easier:

- The Holy Spirit is described as *wind*. "The wind blows wherever it pleases. You hear its sound, but you cannot tell where it comes from or where it is going. So it is with everyone born of the Spirit" (John 3:8).
- The Holy Spirit is like *breath*. "And with that he breathed on them and said, 'Receive the Holy Spirit'" (John 20:22).
- The Holy Spirit is like *oil*. "The Spirit of the Lord is on me, because he has anointed me" (Luke 4:18).
- The Holy Spirit is like a *dove*. "As Jesus was coming up out of the water, he saw heaven being torn open and the Spirit descending on him like a dove" (Mark 1:10).
- The Holy Spirit is like *fire*. "Do not put out the Spirit's fire" (1 Thess. 5:19).
- The Holy Spirit is like a *river*. "'If anyone is thirsty, let him come to me and drink. Whoever believes in me, as the Scripture has said, streams of living water will flow from within him.' By this he meant the Spirit"

(John 7:37–39).

- The Holy Spirit is *power*. "But you will receive power when the Holy Spirit comes on you; and you will be my witnesses in Jerusalem, and in all Judea and Samaria, and to the ends of the earth" (Acts 1:8).

While each of these descriptions discloses an aspect of the Person of the Holy Spirit that is accurate, none are explicitly personal. But don't let that fool you! God the Holy Spirit is just as real a Person as are God the Father and God the Son.

- He has *feelings*, because He is a person. "Do not grieve the Holy Spirit of God" (Eph. 4:30).
- He has a *will*, because He is a person. "All these are the work of one and the same Spirit, and he gives them to each one, just as he determines" (1 Cor. 12:11).
- He *talks and gives assignments*, because He is a person. "The Holy Spirit said, 'Set apart for me Barnabas and Saul for the work to which I have called them'" (Acts 13:2).
- He *pours love into us*, because He is a person. "God has poured out his love into our hearts by the Holy Spirit, whom he has given us" (Rom. 5:5).
- He *helps us in our weakness*, because He is a person. "The Spirit helps us in our weakness" (Rom. 8:26).
- He *prays for us*, because He is a person. "We do not know what we ought to pray for, but the Spirit himself intercedes for us with groans that words cannot express" (Rom. 8:26).
- He *counsels us*, because He is a person. "But the Counselor, the Holy Spirit, whom the Father will send in my name, will teach you all things and will remind you of everything I have said to you" (John 14:26).

Embracing the reality of the Person of the Holy Spirit is vital to encountering the manifest presence of God. The better we know Him, the more effectively we encounter Him.

Let's look more closely at how the Holy Spirit manifests Christ.

Filled with Fire

As incredible as it is that the Person of the Holy Spirit of God lives invisibly inside every believer, we are constantly relating to Him in one way or another. Like having an invisible roommate, our relationship with Him is determined by how well we spot His activity, listen for His voice, respond to His words, recognize His presence and follow His lead. Since God chose to send His Spirit to dwell in us, we want to do everything we can to make Him feel right at home. To do this effectively, we have God the Holy Spirit working on our behalf. It is not rocket science. He has given us three simple and yet highly significant guidelines.

Obey His motivating influence. We are told, "Do not put out the Spirit's fire" (1 Thess. 5:19). To put it another way, "Do not suppress the Spirit" (MSG) or "Do not stifle the Holy Spirit" (NKJV). Embedded in this central instruction is a list of specific activities toward which the indwelling Person of the Holy Spirit is consistently motivating us:

Be joyful always. (1 Thess. 5:16)

Pray continually. (1 Thess. 5:17)

Give thanks in all circumstances. (1 Thess. 5:18)

Test everything. (1 Thess. 5:21)

Hold on to the good. (1 Thess. 5:21)

These are all activities that God's Spirit empowers us to accomplish. Like a fire in our engine, the Holy Spirit motivates us to rejoice, pray, give thanks, test what is true and hold on to what is good. There is no need to fan the flame of the indwelling Holy Spirit, as He doesn't need our help. He does, however, want our cooperation. When we fail to obey the motivating influence of the Holy Spirit, it is possible for us to suppress, stifle, quench or even put out the Spirit's fire and influence. On the other hand, the more we obey the Holy Spirit when He prompts us, the hotter His fire burns in us. God gives the Holy Spirit to those who obey Him (see Acts 5:32). What is impossible to us, apart from God's supernatural intervention, suddenly becomes possible the moment we obey Him. As Charles Spurgeon said, "The Lord teaches us to pray in earnest. May he send his own fire and the heavenly flame of his Spirit, the spirit of grace and supplication, that saints may know how to pray, for we must have the fire with the incense."[79]

Obey His restraining influence. We are told, "Do not grieve the Holy Spirit" (Eph. 4:30). Other translations say, "Do not bring sorrow to God's Holy Spirit," (NLT) and, "Don't grieve God. In other words, don't break His heart. His Holy Spirit is moving and breathing in you. He is most intimately making you fit for Himself. Don't take such a gift for granted" MSG). Also embedded in this instruction is a list of activities from which the indwelling Person of the Holy Spirit is consistently seeking to restrain us:

Do not let the sun go down while you are still angry. (Eph. 4:26)

Do not give the devil a foothold. (Eph. 4:27)

Steal no longer. (Eph. 4:28)
Do not let any unwholesome talk come out of your mouths. (Eph. 4:29)

Get rid of all bitterness, rage and anger, brawling and slander, along with every form of malice. (Eph. 4:31)

While we do not have the power on our own to resist the devil, the Person of the Holy Spirit supernaturally restrains us from evil and empowers us to obey God. If, however, we disobey God and fail to follow His restraint, we bring Him sorrow. While He won't remove His presence, He will, to some extent, remove His influence. Our disobedience will not damage His indwelling presence, but it will affect His manifest presence.

These two instructions—do not *quench* the Holy Spirit and do not *grieve* the Holy Spirit—represent two sides of the same coin. To quench is to *not do* what the Holy Spirit is seeking to motivate you to do. To grieve is to *do* what the Holy Spirit is seeking to restrain. Both reveal the tangible relationship between the indwelling presence of God and His manifest presence. Because His Spirit dwells within us, God is consistently on hand to manifest His presence at any time by exerting His influence both in motivating us to good activity and in restraining evil.

Be filled. When the Bible says, "Be filled with the Spirit" (Eph. 5:18), it is speaking to Christians in the church who already have the indwelling presence. We are now being offered His fullness—the same Holy Spirit but in a fuller manifestation. "Be filled" is a present, imperative, aorist, passive verb in the Greek language. Let me break this down:

- Present tense— An ongoing, continuous action
- Imperative tense—A command or instruction, like "Sit down"
- Aorist tense—An action without regard to time or duration
- Passive voice—An action that is done to us, not one that we initiate

Put it all together, and the words "Be filled" are perhaps more accurately translated "Be being filled" with the Holy Spirit. Be filled initially and progressively—continually. Allow the action, the filling, to be done to you. Like wading into the waters of immersion baptism, we may get in the water under our own power, but we don't baptize ourselves. It is the minister who performs the baptism, lowering us under the water and then lifting us up. The same is true of the Holy Spirit. We say yes to His invitation and wade into His waters, so to speak. It is Christ who is the baptizer or filler in the Holy Spirit.[80]

Christ immerses us in the waters of the Holy Spirit and saturates every area of our lives. Every cell in our body is consumed with His holy presence so that He then can conspicuously manifest Christ to us and through us. This is normally where the rub comes. The biggest hindrance to the infilling of the Holy Spirit is not a theological issue; it is a control issue. Make no mistake about it. To be filled with the Holy Spirit is to be controlled by the Holy Spirit. If we are not willing to give Him control, we forfeit the treasure of His fullness.

The books of Romans and Galatians contain crystal-clear teaching on what it is to be controlled by the Holy Spirit in contrast to being controlled by the sinful nature: "The mind of sinful man is death, but the mind controlled by the Spirit is life and peace" (Rom. 8:6).

Bottom line: "Those controlled by the sinful nature cannot please God" (Rom. 8:8). The war is on. The options are clear. The choice is ours. The appeal has been made: "So I say, live by the Spirit, and you will not gratify the desires of the sinful nature. For the sinful nature desires what is contrary to the Spirit, and the Spirit what is contrary to the sinful nature. They are in conflict with each other, so that you do not do what you want. . . . The one who sows to please his sinful nature, from that nature will reap destruction; the one who sows to please the Spirit, from the Spirit will reap eternal life" (Gal. 5:16–17; 6:8).

Warning: do not dumb down the infilling of the Holy Spirit. Don't swallow shallow theology when it comes to the Person and the work of the Holy Spirit. We don't need *The Holy Spirit for Dummies*. We may be dummies, but we need the flames, not the fumes.

Question: Are your Holy Spirit receivers functioning properly?

John the Baptist promised that Christ would saturate us with the Holy Spirit and with fire (see Matt. 3:11). Be clear. This is a baptism, an immersion. We don't want to settle for a little sprinkling; we want to be fully immersed.

As we have learned, the Holy Spirit is the divine Person who makes Christ known to us. The fire is the manifest presence of Christ which was first fully revealed at Pentecost to the early disciples and is just as available to us today. As post-Pentecost Peter guaranteed, "The promise is for you and your children and for all who are far off—for all whom the Lord our God will call" (Acts 2:39).

To be baptized in the Holy Spirit is to be filled with the Person who glorifies Christ and makes His manifest presence known to us. As we have learned, fire represents the manifest presence of God. Even at Pentecost, the flames around the heads of all the believers visually illustrated for us God's presence in a tangible way.

Once again, let's go back to John and his encounter with Christ that began the book of the Revelation. This I-was-in-the-Spirit moment took John off the bench and got him back in the game. He had been sidelined in exile as a political prisoner, but he wasn't anymore. Strange and wonderful things were about to happen. All kinds of unexpected, out-of-the-box signs and wonders were about to break loose. "I was in the Spirit" was for John. It's for us too.

It is our inheritance. If it is your desire, hold out your hands to Him now and receive:

> *Spirit of God, come. I wade in the waters of Your presence. I relinquish control to You. I yield my rights and privileges to You. Take me and fill me. Take control of my mind, will and emotions. Take control. Baptize me. Immerse me. Saturate me. Spirit, soul and body. Take control. Take back from the enemy any ground I have given over. Father, right now I receive the fullness of the Holy Spirit in the name of the Lord Jesus Christ. Amen.*

If you prayed that prayer—more importantly if you received—take time right now to praise and worship God.

God on Fire in History

Jonathan Edwards's wife, Sarah Pierpont Edwards, was a remarkable person in her own right. Like her husband, she too encountered God's manifest presence and wrote about it very vividly.

I fell into great flow of tears, and could not forbear weeping aloud. It appeared certain to me that God was my Father, and Christ my Lord and Savior, that he was mine and I his. Under a delightful sense of the immediate presence and love of God, these words seemed to come over and over in my mind. "My God, my all; my God, my all." The presence of God was so near, and so real, that I seemed scarcely conscious of anything else. God, the Father and the Lord Jesus Christ seemed as distinct persons, both manifesting their inconceivable loveliness, and mildness, and gentleness, and their great and immutable love to me. I seemed to be taken under the care in charge of my God and Savior, in an inexpressibly endearing manner; and Christ appeared to me as a mighty Savior, under the character of the lion of the tribe of Judah, taking my heart, with all its corruption, under his care, and putting it at his feet. In all things, which concerned me, I felt myself safe under the protection of the Father. . . . The peace and happiness which I hereupon felt was altogether inexpressible. . . . I seemed to be lifted above earth and hell, out of the reach of everything here below, so that I could look on all the rage and enmity of men. . . . The same time I felt compassion and love for all mankind. . . . I continued in a very sweet and lively sense of divine things, day and night.[81]

I was entirely swallowed up in God, as my only portion, and his honor and glory was the object of my supreme desire and delight. . . . This lively sense of the beauty and excellency of divine things continued during the morning, accompanied with peculiar sweetness and delight. To my own imagination, my soul seemed to have gone out of me to God and Christ in heaven, and to have very little relation to my body. God and Christ were so present to me and so near me, that I seemed removed from myself. . . . I never felt such an entire emptiness of self-love, or any regard to any private, selfish interest of my own. . . . The glory of God seemed the all, and in all, and to swallow up every wish and desire of my heart.[82]

Chapter Takeaways

- If you want to see the manifest presence of Christ, you need to be in the Spirit.
- Embracing the reality of the Person of the Holy Spirit is vital to encountering the manifest presence of Christ.
- Because the Holy Spirit is invisible, we are constantly relating to Him, in one way or the other, as if we have an invisible roommate.
- To quench the Holy Spirit is to *not do* what the Holy Spirit is seeking to motivate you to do.
- To grieve the Holy Spirit is to *do* what He is seeking to restrain you from doing.
- To be filled with the Holy Spirit is to be controlled by the Holy Spirit.
- We don't need *The Holy Spirit for Dummies*.
- To be baptized in the Holy Spirit is to be filled with the Person who manifests God's presence to us.

You can't love the Holy Spirit without loving His sword, the Word of God, the Bible. Though many have focused on the revelatory manifestations of the Holy Spirit to the neglect of the Bible, it's critical that we don't make this same mistake. Virtually every page of the Bible oozes with the manifest presence of Christ.

God's Word on Fire

*If the Christian does not know when God is speaking,
he is in trouble at the heart of his Christian life.*[83]
Henry Blackaby

*You diligently study the Scriptures because you think that by them
you possess eternal life. These are the Scriptures that testify about me.*
John 5:39

THE Bible is the ultimate Facebook. Long before Mark
Zuckerberg and his nearly 900 million participants
existed,[84] God wrote the ultimate Facebook in which we can
not only see ourselves more clearly, but we can also see God
in all His glory.

Many Christians think the Bible was written so that we
might read and study it, as if Bible knowledge is an end to
itself. Not so fast. God had much more in mind when He
inspired its writers. The Bible is designed to lead us to an
encounter with God. A word from God doesn't lead us to an
encounter; it is the encounter. The key to reading the Bible
effectively is to know that it is a means to an end, not an end
in itself. We read the Bible because we love the Author and we
want to get to know Him better. Because of this, it is always
important to know what you are looking for in the text.

My family and I have always enjoyed shelling in southwest

Florida. Every year since I was eighteen months old, we have vacationed on some of the finest shelling beaches anywhere in the world. Over the years, we have learned the fine art of shelling and are able to identify close to one hundred different species of shells. It is fun to be able to distinguish a horse conch from an alphabet cone. Our knowledge and experience serves us well as we walk the water's edge. Other shellers will fill their bucket with bleached-white, broken pieces of generic shells and walk right past the more valuable specimens. I've learned that if you are going to walk the beach shelling, it certainly helps to know what to look out for.

The same is true when it comes to Bible reading. It helps to know what you are looking for. Learning to recognize the manifest presence of God in His Word will help our Bible reading immensely.

I have read the Bible each year cover to cover for twenty years, but when I began to discover the manifest presence of God, it radically changed my Bible reading. Instead of just reading as if I was cramming for the next game of Bible trivia, I began to read to encounter God. When I would encounter God while reading, or when I found someone in the Bible who encountered God's manifest presence, I would write in the margin of my Bible the letters MP. The first year I was modestly impressed with my efforts, as I wrote two hundred MPs in the margin. The next year, as my eye became better trained to recognize God's presence, I marked over a thousand MPs. Recently, I recorded several thousand MPs next to the examples of God's conspicuous, tangible presence. More than simply marking MPs, I have, by the grace of God, been able to consistently encounter God myself in my reading.

So let's spend some time training our eyes. The Bible is full of obvious examples of individuals who expressly encountered the reality of *God on fire*. It is also full of invitations for us to encounter God's manifest presence as well. As Andrew Murray suggests, "Take time. Give God time to reveal himself to you. Give yourself time to be silent and quiet before him, waiting to receive, through the Spirit, the assurance of his presence with you, his working in you. Take time to read his word as in his presence, that from it you may know what he asks of you and what he promises you. Let the word create around you . . . [and] within you a holy atmosphere, a holy heavenly light, in which your soul will be refreshed and strengthened for the work of daily life." [85]

Like looking for shells on the beach, we each should want to learn more about what we are looking for as we read our Bibles.

People on Fire

Let's start with Enoch. Enoch not only knew the manifest presence of God, he loved it! He was the great-great-great-great-grandson of Adam and Eve. More importantly, he experientially knew the manifest presence of God so intimately that the record shows, "Enoch walked with God; then he was no more, because God took him away" (Gen. 5:24). A member of the all-star team of faith, the book of Hebrews says of him, "By faith Enoch was taken from this life, so that he did not experience death; he could not be found, because God had taken him away. For before he was taken, he was commended as one who pleased God" (Heb. 11:5). Enoch pleased God because he cherished God's manifest presence. He clearly took the lifestyle of living in God's presence to a whole new level. The New Testament takes this example of Enoch and makes this man a role model for all of us, as the next sentence in Hebrews 11 says: "Without faith it is impossible to please God, because anyone who comes to him must believe that he exists and that he rewards those who earnestly seek him" (Heb.11:6). There is nothing more pleasing to God than the person who seeks His manifest presence.

Cain was the son of Adam and Eve. He is a powerful example of a man who walked away from the manifest presence of God. When God asked him point blank, "Where is your brother Abel?" (Gen. 4:9), he was clearly able to recognize God's voice. He knew immediately who was posing the question and precisely what God was asking. It is also obvious that Cain knew the manifest presence of God, because when the conversation was over, the Bible says, "So Cain went out from the LORD's presence" (Gen. 4:16). Cain was obviously not walking away from the omnipresence of God, because you can't move closer or farther from God's everywhere-presence. Cain was turning his back on God's tangible presence, and he knew it. Sad.

The prophet Elijah lived in a day in which there were numerous altars and prayer meetings but no fire. He knew that his God specialized in sending the fire of His manifest presence, and yet his nation was suffering due to the absence of God's fire and its allegiance to other gods. He challenged the people to a showdown. "You build your altar, prepare your sacrifice and call on your god. I will build my altar, prepare my sacrifice and call on my God. And the god who answers by fire, he is God." The account in First Kings 18 is invigorating, to say the least.

After three strenuous hours, the prophets of Baal were sweaty, bloody, out of breath and out of excuses. Now it was Elijah's turn. He built his altar, prepared the sacrifice and prayed a simple, straightforward prayer: "O LORD, God of Abraham, Isaac and Israel, let it be known today that you are God in Israel and that I am your servant and have done all these things at your command. Answer me, O LORD, answer me, so these people will know that you, O LORD, are God, and that you are turning their hearts back again" (1 Kings 18:36–37). While Elijah never explicitly asked for fire, he didn't need to. He'd asked for God to manifest Himself. This is what happened: "Then the fire of the LORD fell and burned up the sacrifice, the wood, the stones and the soil, and also licked up the water in the trench" (1 Kings 18:38).

When the fire of God's tangible presence falls, it does three things that can only be accomplished by fire: (1) It puts God's *people* in their place. Instantly they fell flat on their faces (see 1 Kings 18:39). (2) It puts *God* in His place. The people erupted in praise declaring, "The LORD—he is God! The LORD—he is God!" (1 Kings 18:39). (3) It puts the *devil* in his place. They seized the prophets of Baal and let none of them escape (1 Kings 18:40). The problem in Elijah's day was never the presence of evil but the absence of the fire of God's manifest presence.

Time and space do not permit us to investigate the plentitude of encounters with God's manifest presence recorded in the Bible. I encourage you to look up these breathtaking, life-changing accounts in your leisure: Noah (see Gen. 5–7), his family (see Gen. 5–9), Abraham (see Gen. 12–25), Lot (see Gen. 19), Isaac (see Gen. 21–28), Jacob (see Gen. 27–49), Joseph (see Gen. 37–50), Moses (see Exod. 3–20), Aaron (see Num. 17), Balaam (see Num. 22–24), Joshua (see Josh. 1–10), Deborah (see Judg. 4–5), Gideon (see Judg. 6–8), Samson (see Judg. 13–16), Samuel (see 1 Sam. 1–3), David (see 1 Sam. 16–17; 2 Sam. 1–2, 6–10), Solomon (see 1 Kings 8–9; 2 Chron. 5–7), Elisha (see 2 Kings 2–8), Hezekiah (see 2 Kings 18–20), Josiah (see 2 Kings 22–23; 2 Chron. 34–35), Jehoshaphat (see 2 Chron. 20), Ezra and Nehemiah (see Neh. 8–9), Job (see Job 38–42), Jeremiah (see Jer. 1), Ezekiel (see Ezek. 1–3), Daniel and his three friends (see Dan. 3, 6–11) and Jonah (see Jon. 1–4).

Every one of these people encountered *God on fire*.

Promises on Fire

In addition to the people in the Bible who encountered the flaming reality of God's manifest presence, there are also promises of God that are strategically designed to lead us into an encounter with His presence. Please resist the urge to take only a glance at these verses and then skip to the next session. Any one of these scriptures—and there are thousands more ready to be unveiled to you—have enough C-4 explosive to ignite a fire in your soul.

"For where two or three come together in my name, there am I with them" (Matt. 18:20). Many sincere Christians have prayed this verse as an omnipresence promise, but it is not. We can gather together in the name of Buddha, Krishna or Mohammad, and God's omnipresence will be there. This potent promise is assuring us that Jesus will conspicuously show Himself when we gather corporately together in His name. Guaranteed.

"Come near to God and he will come near to you" (James 4:8). These words could not refer to God's omnipresence, because it is impossible to get any closer or any farther from His omnipresence. Whenever the Bible uses words to describe movement in proximity to God, it is always referring to His manifest presence. God commits Himself by His Word to the fact that when we genuinely approach God, He will reciprocate. Guaranteed.

"Seek the LORD while he may be found; call on him while he is near" (Isa. 55:6). We are encouraged hundreds of times in the Bible to seek God. Each time it is in reference to His manifest presence. "While He may be found" and "while he is near" could not possibly be referring to God's omnipresence; as we have said, only His manifest presence can be found.

"You will seek me and find me when you seek me with all your heart" (Jer. 29:13). This verse adds a significant principle. In addition to promising His manifest presence to those who seek Him, God is looking for wholehearted seekers. He wants us to be all in. In reality, full-throttle seeking is the only appropriate approach we can take to God's manifest presence, because when we truly comprehend the value of His presence, we won't need anyone prodding us. Our passion to pursue Him will accelerate naturally.

"Here I am! I stand at the door and knock. If anyone hears my voice and opens the door, I will come in and eat with him, and he with me" (Rev. 3:20). This scripture promise is most helpful when we don't know exactly how to pray. Just keep it simple. Open the door to Christ, and welcome His manifest presence. While this verse is commonly applied to pre-Christians for salvation, it is more explicitly an invitation to throw open the door and welcome the conspicuous presence of Christ. Jesus is, after all, speaking these words. The same Jesus who appeared to John in the first chapter of the book of the Revelation is now speaking to the church in the third chapter. He is offering to reveal Himself. Can we even imagine the ascended, glorified, all-potent Christ offering to come into our lives the same way He manifested Himself to John on the island of Patmos? This is precisely what is being offered, not only to the believers in the first century, but to us in the twenty-first century. Jesus is, after all, still walking in the middle of the flame holders, checking the intensity of the fire of His manifest presence that burns in each congregation. We don't need to settle for a flicker when God is on fire. Ole Hallesby wrote in his classic book *Prayer* about this very promise of Revelation 3:20. He highlighted the fact that we have made prayer far too complex, when it is essentially quite simple—just open the door to Christ. God will do the rest. When it is all said and done, prayer is much more about what God does than what we do anyway. Once we as gatekeepers open the door to Christ, there is no limit to what He is capable of doing as He manifests His presence to us.

"If you then, though you are evil, know how to give good

gifts to your children, how much more will your Father in heaven give the Holy Spirit to those who ask him!" (Luke 11:13). Jesus guarantees that when we ask the Father for the Person of the Holy Spirit, He will give us the Person of the Holy Spirit. There are no hidden loopholes or fine print. There need be no bells and whistles. This potent promise is worth cashing in on. When Evan Roberts prayed this verse with hundreds of Welsh believers in 1904, God answered their request. It was the catalyst for the Welsh revival. What will happen when we bank on it?

"If anyone is thirsty, let him come to me and drink. Whoever believes in me, as the Scripture has said, streams of living water will flow from within him.' By this he meant the Spirit, whom those who believed in him were later to receive" (John 7:37–39). Thirst for God is already the work of God. Remember, our craving for God's manifest presence is dead and buried. When it awakens, there is only one explanation. God has raised it from the dead. He is up to something. For this reason, Jesus guarantees us that when we hunger and thirst for God, we will be filled. He will not leave us empty. When He awakens the craving, He will also satisfy the craving. When we encounter His manifest presence, we get more than we bargained for; we get to live in the overflow of His presence as the river of His living water, the Holy Spirit, overflows from our inner being.

"I baptize you with water for repentance. But after me will come one who is more powerful than I, whose sandals I am not fit to carry. He will baptize you with the Holy Spirit and with fire" (Matt. 3:11). The promise to be baptized in the Holy Spirit and in fire is for all Christians. Unfortunately, the word "baptize" has become formalized and carries with it some excess religious baggage. Originally, to baptize meant to saturate, immerse or submerge. It was a commercial word, describing clothes that had been thoroughly drenched in dye. Ships that were sunk at sea were baptized. In the case of Scripture, God promises to saturate or submerge us in the Holy Spirit and in the fire of God's manifest presence. He wants every area of our lives and every cell of our body dripping with His presence and fully under His influence.

"I keep asking that the God of our Lord Jesus Christ, the glorious Father, may give you the Spirit of wisdom and revelation, so that you may know him better" (Eph. 1:17). As Paul prayed for the Ephesian believers, he passionately wanted them to know Christ better. He realized that there was only one way for that to happen: God had to do it. More specifically, God would need to do it the way He always does it: by first giving them the Holy Spirit who is "the Spirit of wisdom and revelation." This high-octane promise is worth using for yourself, your family and your community of faith.

Christ in the Word

The Bible is not an end in itself. It is not good enough to just read and study it. When we stop short of encountering God, we stop too soon. "These are the Scriptures," Jesus said, "that testify about me" (John 5:39). Andrew Murray carried this same burden for the church over one hundred years ago. "Information is the fuel without which the fire cannot burn," he writes. "Fuel is not fire and cannot of itself create fire; but where there is fire, fuel is indispensable to keep it burning, and to make it burn with greater intensity."[86]

When Jesus rose from the dead and talked incognito with two people on the Israeli road to Emmaus, the record shows the following: "And beginning with Moses and all the Prophets, he explained to them what was said in all the Scriptures concerning himself" (Luke 24:27). Jesus conducted a traveling, impromptu Bible study from what is now often referred to as the dry parts of the Bible: the books of Genesis, Exodus, Leviticus, Numbers and Deuteronomy as well as the seventeen books of prophecy. As the two people walked away, they said to each other, "Were not our hearts burning within us while he talked with us on the road and opened the Scriptures to us?" (Luke 24:32). The "hearts burning within us" was evidence that these men had encountered the flaming presence of God as a result of their Christ-led Bible study. This is, to some extent, what should take place every time we read God's Word. We all need more hearts-burning-within-us moments in our Bible reading. It's all too easy to have knowledge but to lack revelation; to know God in principle but never to know Him in Person; to know the omnipresence of God but never to encounter the manifest presence.

You may say to yourself, *I can understand how Moses and Abraham, Enoch and Elijah, Isaiah and Malachi met God on fire, but I am just an ordinary guy.* The record shows us that Moses and the rest of our all-star list were just ordinary guys until they met God. The Bible is full of ordinary people whose lives became extraordinary once they encountered God. Read about Rahab the prostitute (see Josh. 2:1–21; 6:25), Ruth the widow-bride (see Ruth 1–4) and Esther the orphan child (see Esther 1–10).

You might even look at Elijah and shrug your shoulders, thinking, *I could never pray like that. I could never pray down fire. I have nothing in common with Elijah.* That may be how you feel, but that is not what the Bible says. The book of James refers to Elijah as "a man just like us" (James 5:17). You may not feel like Elijah, but Elijah was just like you. Here's a prayer that can help express your Elijah-like faith:

> *Father, as I read the Bible, I want to get to know You, the Author. Give me Your Holy Spirit of wisdom and revelation so that I may know You better and better and better. Open my eyes that I may recognize You as I read. Open my ears that I may hear Your voice, in the name of the Lord Jesus Christ,*

the Word of God.

God on fire encounters are not the work of people, but the work of God. For this reason, it doesn't require extraordinary people to encounter Him—it takes an extraordinary God. God's manifest presence makes common people uncommon. His presence takes ordinary lives like ours and makes them extraordinary. The Bible is designed to lead you to just such an encounter with God.

God on Fire in History

It is almost impossible to overestimate the impact of John Wesley. As a young man, he came to saving faith in the Lord Jesus Christ, and he wrote about it, saying, "I felt my heart strangely warmed; I felt I did trust Christ alone for salvation." From that moment on, the due-north on the compass of his soul was the manifest presence of God.

New Year's Eve is remembered by each of us for many things, but it will be remembered by George Whitefield, John Wesley, Charles Wesley and about sixty others who gathered for a night of prayer as Pentecost—the night the Holy Spirit came powerfully to them. In the wee hours of 1738, they encountered the presence of God like they never had before. John Wesley later wrote, "About three in the morning, as we were continuing instant in prayer, the power of God came mightily upon us, insomuch that many cried out for exceeding joy, and all fell to the ground. As soon as we recovered a little from the awe and amazement at the presence of His Majesty, we broke out with one voice, 'We praise Thee, O God. We acknowledge Thee to be the Lord.'" Five consecutive back-to-back all-night prayer meetings followed, and for the next one hundred years, all-night prayer meetings would characterize Methodism.[87]

Wesley benefited greatly from the core values of the German Pietists. Small-group discipleship became the structure of the early Methodist church. Prayer that was focused on world evangelism characterized their all-night prayer meetings. Wesley, Whitefield and others went on short-term missions. Christian hymnology was taken to a whole new level by John and even more by his brother, Charles Wesley. The social action of John Wesley was impressive. He visited inmates in prison, established orphanages and educated all children equally. History confirms that Wesley teamed up with William Wilberforce to rid slavery from England.

Despite being only five feet, three inches tall and weighing a mere one hundred twenty eight pounds, Wesley was a giant in faith. Historians estimate that Wesley traveled nearly 250,000 miles, mostly on horseback, preached over 40,000 sermons and wrote approximately 250 books and tracts. He often wrote his sermons on horseback, using his saddle as his mobile library. By his death in 1791, there were 79,000 Methodists in England and over 119,000 around the world. Within 110 years there were nearly 90,000 churches with members, scholars and adherents numbering 40 million.[88] This extraordinary impact can all be traced back to the Methodist Pentecost and to these men's encounter with the manifest presence of God.

Chapter Takeaways

- The Bible is the ultimate Facebook.
- A word from God doesn't *lead* us to an encounter; it *is* the encounter.
- Learning to recognize the manifest presence God in His Word will help our Bible reading immensely.

- The Bible is not an end in itself; it is designed to lead us to an encounter with God.

Let's face it. Encountering the manifest presence of God is initially intimidating. Overwhelming. It causes every insecurity inside us to rise to the surface. Ultimately, however, it is the most freeing, cleansing, liberating place we can be. The next step for us to discover is what it truly means to fear the Lord so that we might walk in freedom like we never dreamed possible.

Freed and on Fire

A flame of fire! It is a perpetual fire; a constant fire; a continual burning; a holy, inward flame; which is exactly God's Son was in the world. God has nothing less for us than to be flames![89]
Smith Wigglesworth

Do not be afraid.
Revelation 1:17

THE fear of God is one of the most important and yet least understood realities of the Christian life. There is perhaps nothing else the Bible teaches so extensively that is understood so little.

When you begin to encounter the blazing fire of God's manifest presence, the fear of God is unavoidable. What you previously speculated or theorized about is now breathing down your neck. All your preconceived ideas are burned to ashes the moment you encounter Christ.

The manifest presence of God can be intimidating. Overwhelming. When you think about what is taking place—that you are coming face to face, eyeball to eyeball with Almighty God—of course it will be overwhelming, scary! It was intimidating to John, and he knew Jesus as well as anyone on earth did. When the apostle first saw the exalted, conquering Christ, he was so shocked, so aghast, that when he fell paralyzed at Christ's feet, some of the first words Jesus told him were, "Do not be afraid" (Rev. 1:17). John was understandably shaken. Who could blame him? He felt shock and awe, as did countless others like him throughout both biblical and contemporary history when encountering the presence of God. Jesus' command to "not be afraid" is a common theme in Scripture.

When Abraham encountered God, he was told, "Do not be afraid" (Gen. 15:1; 26:24).

When Israel encountered God, the people were told, "Do not be afraid" (Exod. 20:20).

When Gideon encountered God, he was told, "Do not be afraid" (Judg. 6:23).

When Mary encountered the angel of God, she was told, "Do not be afraid" (Luke 1:30).

John is in good company. It is a pattern that I have observed firsthand in my own life and in the lives of others around the world. When we encounter the penetrating, invasive confrontational presence of God, we are forced to confront the reality of the fear of God on a level that we could never have been prepared for. It is more than psychological or emotional. The Holy Spirit knows how to sneak past our all too familiar religious routines undetected. Before we know it, He has made it past our defense mechanisms, past our control issues, past our wounds and past our dirty laundry and idols. He's crawled up into our lap and is ready to rip off our masks.

No one does it better.

No one does it faster.

No one does it more lovingly, kindly, compassionately, honestly, forcefully, decisively, cleanly and, most of all, redemptively.

He has done it to me on countless occasions. Just when I think I am above reproach, just when I think I'm beyond His reach or as clean as a whistle, He draws back the curtain a little further and brings to light things that had been hidden. Both in my own life and in others', I have observed this common pattern: we are introduced to a proper understanding of the fear of God in the only environment in which the fear of the Lord makes any sense at all: flat on our faces, smack dab in the middle of the manifest presence of Christ.

Healthy Fear of God

There are two definitions of the fear of God that I have found most profitable. While they sound almost contradictory, they are not at all. They are both accurate and entirely complementary.

> Definition 1: The fear of God is the constant awareness that God is watching and weighing all my actions, words, thoughts and attitudes and that one day I will give an account to Him for them.[90]

> Definition 2: The fear of God is living every day with the goal to please God and feel His pleasure.

These two definitions are both reflected perfectly in Jesus. He lived on earth for thirty-three years with the keen awareness that Father God was holding Him accountable on every level of life. He only wanted to do what He saw the Father doing (see John 5:19). He only wanted to speak the words the Father gave Him (see John 14:10). He only could disciple the followers the Father drew to Him (see John 6:44). He only did the work the Father assigned to Him (see John 17:4). It is no wonder that He delighted in the fear of the Lord! Jesus made it His goal to please the Father. The Bible says of Him that He would, "delight in the fear of the LORD" (Isa. 11:3).

Those who misunderstand the fear of God and tell us that it has no place in a Christian's life forfeit one of the great blessings of Christ. The fear of God is wonderful. It is empowering. The benefits of the fear of the Lord are many and far-reaching:

- It prolongs our days (see Prov. 10:27).
- It gives us strength and confidence (see Prov. 14:26).
- It is a fountain of life (see Prov. 14:27).
- It brings us riches (see Prov. 22:4).
- It brings us honor (see Prov. 22:4).
- It brings us life (see Prov. 22:4).
- It helps us perfect holiness (see 2 Cor. 7:1).
- It helps us submit to each other (see Eph. 5:21).

And the list goes on. We certainly don't want to discard something that is so beneficial. There is something inappropriate about fear, however, that we certainly do want to get rid of. It is no coincidence that when John met Christ in all His glory, he needed to be told those four words, "Do not be afraid." While the healthy fear of God that thrust him on his face was perfectly normal, there was some form of unhealthy fear that was at the same moment being exposed. It is no mere coincidence that Abraham, Gideon, Samuel, Mary and thousands of others like them needed to hear those same four words.

Unhealthy Fears

"Do not be afraid" are four of the most powerful words we will ever hear. They appear over 360 times in the Bible for a reason. As we journey through life, we encounter seemingly insurmountable obstacles and circumstances and, in those moments, we all desperately need to hear those words. Most significantly, however, we need them whenever we encounter the manifest presence of Christ, because in His flaming presence certain fears rise to the surface.

Fear of exposure. Most of us have a fear of being known for who we are. For this reason we hide behind our cover-ups. When we encounter Christ, the light of His presence will expose us for who we really are. Things that were buried years ago or hidden in the closet are now brought into the open. Things we tried to forget are now front and center, with a spotlight shining on them.

Fear of losing control. Encountering God's manifest presence makes sitting in the dentist chair seem like a stroll in the park. It's not necessarily the drilling or the possible injections that frighten us, but it is the unknown that makes the process so unnerving. What is coming next? Where will this take me? All control issues run in the red when we enter the unchartered waters of His presence.

Fear of failure. While God doesn't make us feel like failures, He does bring to light our failures, and that can be intimidating. Broken promises, unfulfilled expectations, failed resolutions and incomplete assignments are things we have in our past and yet would rather avoid.

Fear of rejection. For some of us, the default setting on our relational dial is intuitively programmed toward rejection. *If I am exposed for who I am*, we assume, *if I am shown to be a failure, I will be rejected.* This may run deeper in some than in others, but we all have it somewhere in our DNA.

Fear of abandonment. Even more deeply than rejection we may fear abandonment. We fear being left alone on a doorstep like an orphan is. *If the truth about me were brought to the surface, if you dig deep enough and check my credentials*, we reason, *you would find something that would disqualify me and throw me out.* More than rejection, some of us fear abandonment.

Fear of condemnation. The ultimate abandonment is condemnation, the fear of judgment or eternal abandonment. If we are not careful, our fears will keep us at arms' length from God. Deep down we may not want to get too close. Who wants to face all those fears buried down deep in our souls?

The reason God says *do not be afraid* to those who encounter the manifest presence of God is because it is only in His presence that our fears are fully exposed. Dealing with these fears appropriately, fully, decisively, is the key to moving forward with God. Fully embracing the fear of the Lord is the make-it-or-break-it issue of living in the manifest presence of Christ. *Do not be afraid* is the key to delighting in the fear of the Lord the way Jesus did (see Isa. 11:1). *Do not be afraid* are four good words designed to spoon off the surface of our lives the impurities that rise up from deep within us when the heat of God's manifest presence comes to a boil. God does not put the fears inside us, but His penetrating, invading presence raises them to the surface, revealing what is already inside, so that we can overcome them.

The manifest presence of Christ not only reveals Christ, His presence reveals us. "Do not be afraid" is not designed for us to deal with our fear of God but with our fear of ourselves and of who we are without Him. It is only when we embrace the fear of God that we can overcome our fear of ourselves, take off our masks and come out of hiding.

For this reason, the fear of God and humility are forever married. "Humility and the fear of the LORD," the Bible promises, "bring wealth and honor and life" (Prov. 22:4). The most helpful definition of humility I ever heard is this: "Humility is the willingness to be known for who I am." Read that sentence again. When the reality of this truth hits us, it puts a smile on our faces. More significantly, it sets us free.

Dr. Joe Aldrich, former President of Multnomah Bible College, loved the manifest presence of Christ, and he loved creating environments in which he could lead pastors to encounter Christ. He identified the Kingdom principle in Jesus' extensive prayer in John 17: God manifests His presence when believers are in unity. "I have given them the glory that you gave me," Jesus prayed, "that they may be one as we are one: I in them and you in me. May they be brought to complete unity to let the world know that you sent me and have loved them even as you have loved me" (John 17:22–23). In a letter to me, he identified this progressive sequence:

> In order to have community, we need unity.
> In order to have unity, we need humility.
> In order to have humility, we need a fresh encounter with the holiness of God.[91]

Psychologists tell us that it is impossible to feel intimate with anyone of whom we are afraid. Fear drives a wedge. It creates a schism. Distance. If we are to love God, we obviously need to address the issue of unhealthy fear. Since the very encounter with God's manifest presence that bring us into deepest intimacy with God is also what stirs up our fears, we want to leverage those moments in order to gain freedom.

When various fears are brought to the surface—the fear of exposure, losing control, failure, rejection—we should seize the moment. Why stay at arm's length from God when He is inviting us to come closer to Him? We have the unique opportunity to lay an ax to the root of a stronghold that may have been the single greatest hindrance to God's authority in our lives.

Even sincere Christians live with a distorted view of a judgmental God who is out to get them. They paint a picture in their minds of a God who is an ogre in the attic. To the other extreme, some believers think they need to throw off the fear of God, like discarding a cast that has been removed from a healed ankle. It's not the fear of God we need to remove but the distorted view of God. Because this pattern is so common for those who encounter God, the Bible deals with it head on. "For you did not receive a spirit that makes you a slave again to fear," God said, "but you received the Spirit of sonship. And by him we cry, 'Abba, Father.' The Spirit himself testifies with our spirit that we are God's children" (Rom. 8:15–16).

The spirit of slavery is a spirit of fear. Slavery invokes forced labor, abusive authoritarianism, inhumane treatment and loveless demands. This is the orphan spirit which is full of abandonment, rejection, competition, insecurity, striving, unworthiness and fear of punishment. The orphan spirit has never learned to trust the father's love.

The opposite of the orphan spirit, or the spirit of slavery, is the Spirit of God. The way we break free from the orphan spirit that is rooted in fear is to encounter our Father's love— to cry out like a child, "Abba! Daddy! Papa! Father God!"

The love of God sets us free from fear. "There is no fear in love," God says. "But perfect love drives out fear, because fear has to do with punishment. The one who fears is not made perfect in love" (1 John 4:18). Legalism, perfectionism and striving are all part of the orphan spirit of fear. These fears of judgment, condemnation, rejection and failure all need to go. The contrast between these unhealthy fears and the fear of God is significant:

Unhealthy Fear	Healthy Fear
Abandonment	Acceptance
Condemnation	Forgiveness
Striving	Resting
Orphan status	Child status
Slavery	Freedom
Forced Labor	Joyful service
Demoralization	Restoration of dignity
Increasing guilt and shame	Removal of guilt and shame
Deceit and hypocrisy, hiding from God	Transparency and integrity, pursuing God
Running from God	Running toward God
Fig leaves	Nakedness without shame
Fearing His rejection	Anticipation of His pleasure
Despising the fear of God	Delighting in the fear of God

At Home in the Fire

There is a defining moment when we choose the fire—not as a rare or random exception but as our life calling. I will never forget being on my face before God in the sands of Dakar, Senegal, the westernmost point of Africa. I was lying flat on the floor with a room full of African pastors. Many were weeping. Some were openly confessing blatant sin. All were tender before God. I had never met any of them before, but we were united like trusted brothers. God spoke to me on that day, in that very moment, and said, "Fred, I have called you to live in the fire. This is where I live, and this is where I want you to spend the rest of your life—in the fire of My all-consuming presence."

I realized instantly that I needed to relinquish my fears. All of them. And I did. I could almost hear the chains hitting the floor as I relinquished control. I can identify with King David who said, "I sought the LORD, and he answered me; he delivered me from all my fears" (Ps. 34:4). Once free from unhealthy fear, we are free to embrace the fear of the Lord. A few sentences later David said, "Fear the LORD, you his saints, for those who fear him lack nothing" (Ps. 34:9).

None fully embraced the fear of the Lord and none enjoyed greater intimacy with the Father than did Jesus. The early Christians similarly walked "in the fear of the Lord and in the comfort of the Holy Spirit" (Acts 9:31, NKJV). The psalmist says that intimacy and the fear of God live together in perfect synergy. "The LORD confides in those who fear him; he makes his covenant known to them" (Ps. 25:14). "But the eyes of the LORD are on those who fear him, on those whose hope is in his unfailing love" (Ps. 33:18).

The fear of God is not for time; it's for eternity. "The fear of the LORD is pure, enduring forever," the psalmist wrote (Ps. 19:9). It is clean and cleansing. The book of Revelation echoes the words, "Fear God" (Rev. 14:7). As New Testament worshipers, we are also told unequivocally to worship God with reverence and awe, for our God is a consuming fire (see Heb. 12:28–29). Let's pray for this very thing:

> *Wow! I choose the fire. I embrace the fear of God. I delight in the fear of God. Bring to the surface any and all of my unhealthy fears. Expose them. Evict them. Displace them with the fear of God. From this day forward, I will, by the grace of God, walk in humility and in the fear of the Lord.*

God on Fire in History

By his twenty-second birthday, the name of George Whitefield was a household word throughout England. He became known as the "fire-bringer." Crowds grew to more than twenty thousand people at a time at his meetings. In Moorfields, England, sixty thousand gathered. Whitefield's preaching was so God empowered that people often fell to the ground under conviction of sin and under the weight of God's tangible presence. Those who heard the Word of God were often so deeply cut to the heart and convicted of personal sin that they would cry out in loud shrieks and agony. Following Whitefield's sermons, people would spend the whole night in public places praying and praising God.

In Scotland crowds were so enthusiastic that they continued until two in the morning. Whitefield said, "Such a commotion was surely never heard of … For about an hour and a half there was such weeping, so many falling into deep distress … that description is impossible. The people seemed to be smitten in scores. They were carried off and brought into the house like wounded soldier taken from a field of battle."[92]

Benjamin Franklin went as a skeptic to hear George Whitefield preach. He stood among the crowd and was so profoundly moved while listening in the open air that he surprised himself, emptying his pockets of all the money he had in order to invest in an orphanage.[93]

Much is made of Whitefield's oratory skills, but pure rhetoric does not bring conviction of sin, deep repentance, faith in Christ and signs and wonders. Let the record show that the Holy Spirit of God encountered those who listened to Whitefield's message. The record should also show that not everyone was approving. Opponents threw stones, dirt rotten eggs and dead cats at him.[94]

Like John Wesley, Whitefield was a man of compassion who visited hospitals, prisons and orphanages. He established Bethesda Orphanage, now the oldest charity in North America. He preached more than eighteen thousand sermons to as many as ten million people. He preached one of his final sermons on the Boston Commons to twenty-three thousand people, the largest single gathering of people up to that point in American history.

Chapter Takeaways

- The manifest presence of God can be intimidating.
- When we encounter the invasive presence of God, we confront the reality of the fear of God.
- The love of God sets us free from unhealthy fear.
- The manifest presence of Christ not only reveals Christ, His presence reveals us. "Do not be afraid" is not designed for us to deal with our fear of God but our fear of ourselves.
- Only when we embrace the fear of God can we overcome the fear of ourselves.

- The fear of God is not for time—it's for eternity.

Once we face our fears and learn to not only live in the fire of God's manifest presence but to love it, we will begin to delight in the fear of the Lord the way Jesus did. We will also begin to delight in His name. Let's learn how His name communicates His presence.

10

God's Name on Fire

*There are occasions when for hours I lay prostrate before God
without saying a word of prayer or a word of praise—
I just gaze on Him and worship.*[95]
A.W. Tozer

I am the Living One.
Revelation 1:18

THE name of God is priceless. His name is as good as His
character. It represents His nature, His worth, His identity
and His very being. The names of God are not nicknames
given to Him by people. God had no father or mother or
great-aunt to name Him. His names were given to Him by
Himself, and they are made known to us as a means by which
He wants us to come to know Him. His names communicate
His manifest presence. To truly discover a name of God is to
encounter Him by experience. His names communicate His
manifest presence, so to truly understand a name of God is to
encounter God.

When Atlanta real estate mogul Bill Johnson purchased
the aging Ritz-Carlton Hotel in Boston in 1983 for
approximately $70 million, people thought he was crazy.
What the critics didn't realize is that he was not after that one
hotel—he wanted the name. Ritz-Carlton was synonymous

with excellence. With the purchase of the real estate property, Johnson acquired the rights to the trademark, logo and name of Ritz-Carlton. Mr. Johnson wanted to build an international luxury hotel conglomerate that would redefine hospitality all over the world. The Ritz-Carlton's standard white-tie and apron uniforms for staff, fresh-cut flowers, signature cobalt-blue drinking goblets and classy logo with a lion and crown all came with their name. The name Ritz-Carlton meant 100 percent customer satisfaction, and this lived up to their motto that says, "We are ladies and gentlemen serving ladies and gentlemen."[96] Bill Johnson knew the value of a name, and he was willing to pay for it.

If the name Ritz-Carlton was worth millions, it would be impossible for us to put a value on the name of God. As we pursue the manifest presence of God, we will want to learn more about the value of His name.

The names of God reveal His character, His virtue, His worth and His Person. The names of God found in the Bible are accurate manifestations of the living God to real people in the past for our benefit in the present. While all God's names are worth investigating, we will concentrate on the names of God that refer explicitly to His manifest presence.

The Word

John began his Gospel, "In the beginning was the Word, and the Word was with God, and the Word was God" (John 1:1). To avoid any misunderstanding regarding the identity of the person he was referring to as the Word, John quickly added, "The Word became flesh and made his dwelling among us. We have seen his glory, the glory of the One and Only, who came from the Father, full of grace and truth" (John 1:14). When Jesus is identified as the Word, He is clearly defined as the expression of God's essence, the One who communicates

God to us, the second Person of the triune God in whom we can uniquely see the glory of God Himself.

When John saw this same Jesus in the book of the Revelation, he wrote, "Out of his mouth came a sharp double-edged sword" (Rev. 1:16). This word picture of a sword corresponds to the Word of God being referred to elsewhere in the Bible as "the sword of the Spirit" (Eph. 6:17; see also Heb. 4:12). Toward the culmination of the book of the Revelation, we see the return of the triumphant Christ in vibrant detail:

> I saw heaven standing open and there before me was a white horse, whose rider is called Faithful and True. With justice he judges and makes war. His eyes are like blazing fire, and on his head are many crowns. He has a name written on him that no one knows but he himself. He is dressed in a robe dipped in blood, and his name is the Word of God. The armies of heaven were following him, riding on white horses and dressed in fine linen, white and clean. Out of his mouth comes a sharp sword with which to strike down the nations. 'He will rule them with an iron scepter.' He treads the winepress of the fury of the wrath of God Almighty. On his robe and on his thigh he has this name written: KING OF KINGS AND LORD OF LORDS. (Rev. 19:11–16)

The Word who created the world in the beginning and who, as noted above, returns to rule over the world in the end is the same Word who communicates God's presence to us in the meantime.

The Light

John records in his Gospel the memorable words of Jesus, "I am the light of the world" (John 9:5). He also wrote in his first letter, "God is light; in him there is no darkness at all" (1 John

1:5). It is no mere coincidence that the first words we have on record that God spoke were "Let there be light" (Gen. 1:3). God is all about illumination, communication and revelation.

The apostle Paul takes what God did in creation and applies it to what God does in revelation: "For God, who said, 'Let light shine out of darkness,' made his light shine in our hearts to give us the light of the knowledge of the glory of God in the face of Christ" (2 Cor. 4:6). Paul is explicitly taking the tangible impact of God's let-there-be-light declaration at the formation of the physical galaxies and applying it to the less tangible impact of God's let-there-be-light declaration at the manifestation of God's presence to His people.

Consuming Fire

Whether or not we consider consuming fire as a name of God or one of His attributes, it is nevertheless a revelation of who He is. Keep in mind, virtually all light is the result of fire. Moses, who met God in the flaming bush (see Exod. 3:2) and later on the flaming mountain (see Deut. 5:22), declared for all to hear, "The LORD your God is a consuming fire" (Deut. 4:24). The author of the book of Hebrews reinforced this same perspective to his New Testament Christian audience by writing, "Let us be thankful, and so worship God acceptably with reverence and awe, for our 'God is a consuming fire'" (Heb. 12:28–29).

Looking more closely, we discover that the triune God—Father, Son and Holy Spirit—is on fire. God the Father is called a consuming fire (see Deut. 4; Heb. 12). God the Son is shown to be on fire in the book of the Revelation. God the Holy Spirit is said to also be on fire, and we are told not to extinguish Him (see 1 Thess. 5:19). As we have shown, fire is frequently used in the Bible to refer to God's manifest presence. The fact that God is a consuming fire provides further evidence that this characteristic is embedded deep in His character.

I AM

When unsuspecting Moses met *God on fire* in a bush, he asked God the logical question at point-blank range, "What is Your name? Who shall I tell them sent me?" (Exod. 3:10–14). God responded with the defining words, "I AM WHO I AM" (Exod. 3:14). This is the Hebrew word hayah, which means "to be, become, exist." It is an intransitive verb, meaning it has no direct object; it is absolute, complete in itself. The Hebrew name for God is *Yahweh*, which is based on the verb "to be." It represents the perpetual state of uninterrupted existence: I am who I am. I will be who I will be. This name represents the essence of all life and existence. As white light is absolute and complete yet when it goes through a prism will manifest various colors, so the singular name of God, I AM, can be expressed in a multitude of ways. The one true God meets a virtually limitless number of needs. Throughout the Bible God reveals Himself in several Yahweh-based names:

- Yahweh-Jireh, the Lord our provider (Gen. 22:14)
- Yahweh-Rapha, the Lord our healer (Exod. 15:26)
- Yahweh-Nissi, the Lord our banner (Exod. 17:15)
- Yahweh-M'kaddesh, the Lord who makes us holy (Lev. 20:8)
- Yahweh-Shalom, the Lord our peace (Judg. 6:24)
- Yahweh-Tsidkenu, the Lord our righteousness (Jer. 33:16)
- Yahweh-Rohi, the Lord our shepherd (Ps. 23:1)
- Yahweh-Shammah, the Lord who is there (Ezek. 48:35)

- Yahweh-Sabaoth, the Lord of hosts (Ps. 46:7; Isa. 1:24, NKJV)

Jesus used this same phrase "I am" to refer to Himself on numerous occasions. Bible scholars have shown that these "I am" statements are unique to Christ. None of Jesus' contemporaries used this phrase. In the Greek language Jesus said "Ego-eimi," or literally, "I, I am." It was an emphatic way of clarifying His unique identity. I am and no one else.

- I am the bread of life (John 6:35). I and no one else will give lasting nourishment.
- I am the gate of the sheep (John 10:7). I and no one else will provide access to home.
- I am the good shepherd (John 10:11, 14). I and no one else will effectively nurture and care for you.
- I am the way (John 14:6). I and no one else will give you access to the Father.
- I am the truth (John 14:6). I and no one else is the ultimate reality.
- I am the life (John 14:6). I am the only One to give life, full and abundantly.
- I am the light of the world (John 8:12). I am the only One to reveal the truth about God.
- I am the resurrection (John 11:25). I am the only One to give eternal life beyond the grave.
- I am the true vine (John 15:1). I am the only One to continuously nourish and revitalize you.
- I am the Alpha (Rev. 1:8). I am the One who initiates everything.
- I am the Omega (Rev. 1:8). I am the One who will culminate everything.
- I am the First (Rev. 1:17). I am the One who set everything in motion.

- I am the Last (Rev. 1:17). I am the One to whom everything will return.
- I am the Living One (Rev. 1:18). I am the only One to whom every living thing owes its existence.

On one notable occasion Jesus simply said, "Before Abraham was born, I am!" (John 8:58), referring to both His own pre-existence and to His indisputable deity. Those who heard Him knew He was calling Himself God and picked up stones to execute Him for blasphemy (see John 8:59).

Each time Jesus said "I am," He was revealing another dimension of God's manifest presence—the aspect of God's character that He intends for us to know by experience. This is perfectly consistent with what the writer of the book of Hebrews said: "In these last days [God] has spoken to us by his Son, whom he appointed heir of all things, and through whom he made the universe. The Son is the radiance of God's glory and the exact representation of his being" (Heb. 1:2–3).

Unknown Name

Toward the culmination of the book of the Revelation, John again saw the magnificent, triumphant Christ (see Rev. 19:11–16). This time, however, Jesus was not walking among the flame holders. He was returning to the earth riding a white horse to confront the injustices of the world, and the massive angelic armies were riding with him. His eyes were still like blazing fire and His royal robe was still flowing. His name was conspicuously defined as Faithful and True as well as the Word of God. Both on His robe, like an embroidered logo, and on His thigh, perhaps like a tattoo, were the larger-than-life names King of kings and Lord of lords.

Nestled unobtrusively in the otherwise dazzling description of Christ is this sentence: "He has a name written on him that no one knows but he himself" (Rev. 19:12). As a

God-encounterer, this has become one of my favorite names for Christ: the unknown name. It humbles me and reminds me that no matter how well I know Him, there is always more. As much as I relish every name that I've come to know by experience, there is more about God that I joyfully pursue. No matter how fully I understand Him, I am barely scratching the surface.

By Experience

The only way to get to know someone is to meet them personally. Reading about people in a book, seeing their names on a mailbox or following them on Twitter is not the same as knowing them. We need to be properly introduced. The only way to truly know God is to know Him by name, and the only way to truly know God by name is to know His name by experience. All the names of God recorded in the Bible were known by someone's experience. None of them are theoretical titles. They are perpetual realities.

Abraham encountered Yahweh-Jireh when the substitute ram providentially appeared in the thicket and he no longer needed to sacrifice his own son, Isaac. Abraham learned God's name Provider by experience (see Gen. 22:1–18).

Moses and his friends encountered Yahweh-Rapha when the bitter waters turned miraculously sweet, and God promised them that He would keep all disease from them. Moses learned God's name Healer by experience (see Exod. 15:26).

Moses and his nation encountered Yahweh-Nissi when they, against all odds, miraculously defeated the Amalekites on the field of battle. Moses learned God's name Victory Banner by experience (see Exod. 17:15).

When the psalmist sang on the street corner his open request, "O magnify the Lord with me, and let us exalt his name together" (Ps. 34:3, RSV), he was hoping to gather a crowd of fellow worshipers to join with him in singing the names of God. Names that the Israelites had learned from experience. Declaring the glory of His name and verbally reflecting the specific ways God has manifested His presence is the essence of true worship.

In a sense, the name of God is a two-way street. God moves in one direction and extends Himself to us. We move in the other direction and respond to Him. Unless we both show up in the same place at the same time, we will not come to know Him.

While God's name is often referenced in the plural, we should affirm that the Bible frequently refers to His name in the singular:

"You shall not take the name of the LORD your God in vain." (Exod. 20:7, NKJV)

"Hallowed be your name." (Matt. 6:9)

It is important to always maintain the singular nature of God. We are monotheists who affirm, "The LORD our God, the LORD is One" (Deut. 6:4). At the same time, we can quickly add that we are trinitarian-monotheists who affirm that our one God has eternally existed in three Persons—Father, Son and Holy Spirit—and each Person is fully God.

This Trinitarian, singular God, like a perfectly cut diamond, is multifaceted. In fact, far more than multifaceted, He is infinitely-faceted. For this reason the infinitely-faceted, triune God has chosen to reveal Himself by a multitude of names in order to reveal His singular Being. He has also chosen to preserve these names in His eternal Word so that we might be able to read them and relate to them and say, "Wow! Me too, Lord. I have come to know You by experience in the same way Jacob or so-and-so did." When God reveals to us one of His names, He is not *preparing* to lead us to an encounter with Himself, He has already done so.

As good as the name Ritz-Carlton may have been, it was not good enough. In the 1990s many of the Ritz-Carlton hotels were not yielding a profit. Some were over financed. When the economy suffered and the real-estate market took a dive, Bill Johnson faced his own challenges. Although Marriott purchased the majority of the Ritz-Carlton hotels and assumed their international debt load, Mr. Johnson had to file for personal bankruptcy to protect his interests.[97]

While Ritz-Carlton illustrates the value of a name, it also illustrates that a name doesn't always live up to its value. God's name, on the other hand, stands alone. There is no way to overestimate its value. "God . . . gave him the name that is above every name, that at the name of Jesus every knee should bow . . . and every tongue confess that Jesus Christ is Lord, to the glory of God the Father" (Phil. 2:9–10).

The very fact that God allows us as His people to experientially know Him by name is proof positive that He manifests His presence. A name discloses who someone is. It represents the character, nature, essence of the person. It is no wonder that God is jealous for us to guard the value of His name.

When God says, "You shall not misuse the name of the LORD your God, for the LORD will not hold anyone guiltless who misuses his name" (Exod. 20:7), He wants us to mean something each time we speak His name. Since the only way to know His name is by experience, every time we use His name, we are to bear witness to His manifest presence.

This is likely why Jesus included in His model prayer the phrase "hallowed be your name" (Matt. 6:9). It is an explicit request for the manifest presence of God, and one we also can pray to the Father.

> *Lord, hallow Your name. Make known to me today the value of Your name by experience. Manifest Your presence in such a way that You lead us into a fresh encounter with You. Through us, Lord, make Your name famous.*

God on Fire in History

Few people have carried the manifest presence of Christ more effectively than William J. Seymour. The Azusa Street Revival that was born in his church has given rise to the modern Pentecostal charismatic movement, which now, only one hundred years later, includes 800 million believers, or half of the body of Christ around the world.

Louisiana-born Seymour was a man of prayer who regularly spent five hours a day in prayer. He was invited by a group of eight other black families to move to California so he could start a prayer meeting in a private home. On one particularly evening, God's manifest presence so filled that entire house that people fell to the ground in repentance and worship. Many people were healed of ailments, and literally everyone who walked near the house would fall to the ground, repent and come to Christ. By the next morning, the city was in such a stir that the crowds were unable to get near the house. They rented a larger building at 312 Azusa Street where they established the Azusa Street Mission (ASM). The tangible presence of God lasted for years there without diminishing.[98]

Though many mainline Protestant leaders did not understand the supernatural phenomena occurring and some questioned his doctrinal distinctives, almost everyone wanted to pray with Seymour. None could find fault with his godly character.

On Maundy Thursday, April 1, 1906, Seymour received his personal Pentecost. Seymour, an African-American, knelt with a white seeker. Douglas Nelson in an autobiography wrote, "Divine love melted his heart; he sank to the floor seemingly unconscious.[99] He later described the experience like a sphere of fiery, white, hot, radiance falling on him malign his heart with divine love."[100]

Interestingly, at first Seymour did not speak in tongues. He wrote, "Tongues are one of the signs . . . but it is not the real evidence of the baptism in everyday life. If you get angry or speak evil or back bite, I care not how many tongues you have, you have not the baptism of the Holy Spirit."[101] For Seymour it was not tongues but love that characterized the true baptism of the Holy Spirit. His pivotal belief was that there must be no color line in the church. As God had blended the cultures at the first Christian Pentecost in Jerusalem, He did something similar on Azusa Street. Even newspapers reported, "Multitudes have come, Ethiopians, Chinese, Indians, Mexican, and other nationalities worship together."[102]

Seymour's newspaper, The Apostolic Faith, grew in circulation from five thousand to fifty thousand. Within two years of its founding, the mission had sent twenty-five missionaries to Liberia, China, Japan, Hong Kong and other nations. Within three years it had churches in over fifty nations from Iceland to Tasmania and had published literature in thirty languages. By 1914 it had representatives in every U.S. city that had a population of three thousand or more.[103] Today the Pentecostal charismatic church is the fastest-growing body of believers on every continent.

Seymour significantly influenced other charismatic leaders, including Charles Mason, founder of the Church of

God in Christ, A.J. Tomlinson, leader of the Church of God in Cleveland, Tennessee and Aimee Semple McPherson, who established the Foursquare Gospel Church.

Chapter Takeaways

- The name of God is priceless.
- To truly discover a name of God is to encounter Him by experience.
- The names of God are not nicknames; His names were given to Him by Himself.

The name of God is potent, or, as the theologians say, "omnipotent" (all-potent). When Christ rose from the dead and ascended into heaven, He sat down on the throne with something in His hands. Let's learn what it means for Christ to hold the keys.

He Holds the Keys

The truth is that even today miracles are being wrought
in the Name of Christ.[104]
Augustine of Hippo

I hold the keys of death and Hades.
Revelation 1:18

KEYS unlock doors, start engines, solve problems, open up new territories and gain us access to untapped resources. Whoever holds the keys to something generally holds the power and authority.

John the apostle was a political prisoner of Rome living on the isolated, abandoned island of Patmos, a place similar to what the island of Alcatraz was like when it hosted maximum-security prisoners. He'd had no visitors in who knows how long. Then suddenly Christ showed up. That experience would have been like being a POW and suddenly, inside your jail cell, having the president of your country appear. John's president was Jesus, and John had been locked up because of his loyal service to the King. Not only did the King appear, but He announced to the prisoner, of all things, "I hold the keys!" (Rev. 1:18).

The Greek word for keys is *kleis* and is used only six times in the New Testament—twice in the Gospels and four times in the book of the Revelation. The word "keys" would have created a vivid word picture for any prisoner. Whether John was behind bars or in leg irons, few words would have encouraged him more than "I have the keys." He already knew, at least in principle, that Jesus had authority over everything. Years earlier, as he had stood with his fellow disciples on the mountain in Galilee, he had heard the recently risen Christ announce, "All authority in heaven and on earth has been given to me" (Matt. 28:18). But this was different. He was facing the exalted Christ, who was standing a few feet from him, saying, as he rested his hand on John's shoulder, "I hold the keys." It was as if Jesus had said, "I not only have authority over your prison term, but I have authority over the entire Roman Empire." Jesus didn't stop there. He went on to declare, "I hold the keys of death and Hades" (Rev. 1:18).

Talk about raising your security clearance.

Someone else had authority over the Roman Empire, namely Caesar, but no one but Jesus had authority over death and Hades—the dormitory, so to speak, for the dead.

So how did He get the keys? In His next phrase Jesus gives the answer: "I am the Living One; I was dead, and behold I am alive for ever and ever!" (Rev. 1:18). He'd entered the realm of death and Hades as a crucified Man, and He'd risen as the conquering hero. He'd grabbed the keys with His own bare hands.

"I hold the keys" and, more explicitly, "I hold the keys of death and Hades" are words on fire. They were first spoken as Jesus walked among the flame holders, revealing His glorious presence. They were and are emboldening. They were and are fearless words; courageous, lion-hearted words. I would submit that the words "I hold the keys" can only be heard in the context of an encounter with the manifest presence of Christ.

It is one thing to sit in a library, reading about the

sovereignty of God from Augustine, Calvin or Karl Barth. It is something entirely different to encounter the exalted Christ standing a few feet from you as He puts His hot hand on your shoulder saying, "I hold the keys."

The phrase "I hold the keys" has everything to do with fulfilling our mission, pioneering new territory and making disciples of all nations. Christ is the chief apostle, and He opens doors that no one can shut and shuts doors no one can open.[105] Doors of missional opportunity are only opened by the Lord of the Harvest and by those who walk in His authority. When we encounter the manifest presence of this same triumphant Christ, He commissions us with all the same I-hold-the-keys authority.

Keys to the Kingdom

Andrew Murray, in a week-long conference with African missionaries in 1901, challenged the group by pinpointing what he labeled "the key to the missionary problem." "Missionaries," he argued, "believe in the presence of the Spirit of God, but they lack the encounter.[106] There never should be a missionary ministry that is not full of the presence of the Lord."[107] His words may have been written one hundred years ago, but they remain cutting-edge relevant today.

Many have documented throughout history the fact that all the great Kingdom-advancing, church-building, nation-discipling leaders and movements were born in an I-hold-the-keys, manifest-presence encounter with God. Murray, however, issued a new directive: the need for a fresh encounter with Christ. He called the missionaries of his day to "a definite consecration; to be filled with the Spirit and the love of Christ."[108]

The African missionaries not only heard Murray's challenge, but they responded wholeheartedly. They met God so deeply that Murray's next words rang with experiential conviction: "The Pentecostal commission can only be carried out by a Pentecostal church in Pentecostal power."[109]

These missionary talks were published in the book *The Key to the Missionary Problem*. It is no surprise that David Bryant, one of the foremost prayer mobilizers and prophets of hope in our generation, reports that this book is one of two that have had the greatest influence in shaping his own thinking. It is perhaps no coincidence that *God on Fire* is being published one hundred years later by the same publishing house that printed Murray's book.

There is a corresponding relationship between encountering the presence of Christ and being empowered to carry out the mission of Christ. Bryant, in his ministry, used these two words: "fullness" and "fulfillment." Fullness refers to what Christ does *in* us, while fulfillment refers to what Christ does *through* us. Fullness is the revival of God's manifest presence in the church; fulfillment is the advancing of Christ's Kingdom in the world.[110] Jonathan Edwards's *An Humble Attempt* is another book that emphasizes this idea of fullness and fulfillment, though in different words. The full title of Edwards's thesis is a bit lengthy but insightful: *An Humble Attempt to Promote Explicit Agreement and Visible Union of God's People in Extraordinary Prayer for the Revival of Religion and the Advancement of Christ's Kingdom on Earth.* Notice the target of Edwards's manifesto to rally the church to pray toward the goals that are irreversibly linked together in the economy of God: revival in the church and advancing Christ's Kingdom in the world.[111]

Lost Keys

There is nothing worse than having misplaced your keys. The feeling of being ready to go but not being able to find the keys is the worst. Tragically, it seems that many Christians and their congregations have lost the keys. They have both abdicated their authority and lost sight of Christ's authority.

The same Christ who came back from the grave with guns blazing, saying "I hold the keys" had announced to His disciples years earlier, "I hand you the keys." Specifically, He had said, "I will give you the keys of the kingdom of heaven; whatever you bind on earth will be bound in heaven, and whatever you loose on earth will be loosed in heaven" (Matt. 16:19). These two declarations are unmistakably similar. Jesus used the same Greek word *kleis* on both occasions. He referred to Hades, or the gates of Hades, on both occasions (see Matt. 16:18; Rev. 1:18). Additionally, both statements involved a defining moment at which His followers encountered the manifest presence of Christ: John while with Jesus on Patmos, and the disciples during Peter's spot-on declaration, "You are the Christ, the Son of the living God" (Matt. 16:16). Jesus immediately pointed out that neither intelligence nor human ingenuity were the source of Peter's declaration but rather the sovereign intervention of God's Holy Spirit providing the disciple supernatural revelation.[112] It is on this rock of the revelation of Christ on which He promised to build His church (see Matt. 16:18). Keep in mind, a revelation of Christ does not lead you to an encounter; it is the encounter with Christ.

Kingdom Keys

The keys Jesus holds out to us as His disciples are Kingdom keys—"keys of the kingdom," as Jesus said (Matt. 16:19). As King of the Kingdom, Jesus commissions us as His followers to join Him in advancing His Kingdom in various ways. Let's look at all the ways we are called to join Him in Kingdom living:

- To pray the Kingdom (see Matt. 6:10)
- To seek the Kingdom (see Matt. 6:33)
- To recognize the Kingdom (see Matt. 13:11)
- To live the Kingdom (see Matt. 13:31)
- To preach the Kingdom (see Matt. 24:14)
- To value the Kingdom (see Matt. 13:44)
- To exercise the authority of the Kingdom (see Matt. 10:7–8)

Now He hands us the keys of the Kingdom.

It is vital for us as Kingdom people to understand the reality of the Holy Spirit in the advancement of the Kingdom. "For the kingdom of God," the Bible says, "is not a matter of eating and drinking, but of righteousness, peace and joy in the Holy Spirit" (Rom. 14:17). The dynamic interrelationship between the Person of the Holy Spirit and the experiential reality of the Kingdom of God has practical significance. Because the Holy Spirit's primary ministry is to make Christ known to us and through us, we recognize that Christ's Kingdom is advanced by the manifestation of Christ's presence. When we pray "Your kingdom come," we are inviting the Holy Spirit to come and manifest Christ.

Every person mightily used of God receives his or her life calling in the fire. Like a Marine's sword, we are thrust into the flames, pounded and galvanized in the white-hot presence of Christ right before we are carried into combat. Even the early disciples, who had been through a three-year intensive discipleship boot camp with Christ, would have failed miserably at their mission if they had not been galvanized in the fires of Pentecost. If they needed the flaming inferno of Christ's manifest presence, so do we. We are not ready to go and make disciples of anyone until we have been filled with His Sprit, set on fire with His presence and convinced that He holds the keys—the keys of authority not only over the visible dominions but also over the invisible. It's important to acknowledge this in our worship and prayer.

Hail to the Chief! The King who holds the keys. All Hail King Jesus! All hail to the power and the dominion of Christ, for Yours is the Kingdom and the power and the glory forever and ever!

We all need our own I-hold-the-keys encounter with the exalted Christ. We all face our own set of issues that challenge the sovereignty of God. The seemingly impossible situations that we currently face suggest to us that not even God is able to do anything to help us. What is it for you? Your job layoff. Your finances. Your marriage. Your future. Your upside-down mortgage. You know that God has called you to serve Him, and yet you feel stuck and don't know how to get out of your difficulty. You know that the Bible says, "Now to him who is able to do immeasurably more than all we ask or even imagine . . ." (Eph. 3:20), yet the circumstances of your life say, "God is not able. No way. Not now. Not ever. He is not able to help."

More important than a quick fix or even a miracle, you need an encounter. You need an I-hold-the-keys encounter.

You need to grab your seemingly impossible circumstances by the throat and say, "Don't look at me that way! Don't tell me that my God is not able. He is too able!" It's a matter of sovereignty. Are your circumstances sovereign, or is the risen exalted Christ sovereign?

When you encounter Christ and have your I-hold-the-keys moment, you will recognize that all bets are off. Nothing is impossible. Everything is instantly possible, because the God who raised Jesus from the dead is standing right in front of you, holding the keys. He came back from the dead holding the keys. This key-holding Christ is the same One who said, "All authority in heaven and on earth has been given to me"

(Matt. 28:18). "All authority" means He has the jurisdiction to change your job situation, your marital situation, your moral situation. Nothing you face that seems impossible to you is impossible to Him. Jesus is the key holder. He is the ultimate game changer.

The first key He wants to use is the key to your heart. He wants to take out your heart of unbelief and fill you with faith. Bottom line, I-hold-the-keys means, "You can trust Me. You can trust Me with anything. Anything."

God on Fire in History

History remembers with great emphasis St. Francis of Assisi for his vow of poverty and his fascination with birds. What history often fails to highlight is that Francis served the poor, healed the sick, spent nights in prayer and prepared the ground for the next generation of reformers.

The first sermon St. Francis preached led his entire congregation to encounter God and set the pattern for Francis's life and ministry. As his influence extended to Europe, the Middle East and India, Francis served the poor, preached Christ and established his followers as the Franciscan Order of Monks. He trained his disciples to spend nights in prayer. Though he lived only forty-five years and was never officially ordained as a priest, he brought the manifest presence of God everywhere he went. He was called "a living sanctuary of the Holy Spirit."[113] His preaching was described as "penetrating the heart like fire."[114]

There are accounts that say the sign of the cross was miraculously burned on his body on September 24, 1122.[115]

Many believe this was God's stamp of ownership and approval on the surprisingly counter-cultural, God-encountering, non-religious life of a simple saint who brought prayer and the Bible back into the hands of everyday people.

The death of St. Francis in 1226 did not mark the end of his impact. Many reformers and revivalists followed in his footsteps, leading the church back to an encounter with the manifest presence of God, including John Tauler (early 1300s), John Wycliffe (mid 1300s) and John Huss (late 1300s). Each of them was a forerunner for Luther, Zwingli and Calvin and for the Reformation that was soon to follow.

Chapter Takeaways

- Whoever holds the keys holds the power.
- When Jesus rose from the dead, He grabbed the keys with His own bare hands.
- When we encounter the manifest presence of God, we are confronted by the same I-hold-the-keys authority that John was.
- The same Christ who said "I hold the keys" says to us, "I hand you the keys."

Christ *holds* the keys, and He *hands* us the keys. He invites us to join Him in opening doors to people to encounter the manifest presence of Christ. When John turned to see the voice speaking to him, even before he saw Jesus he saw the flame holders. Flame holders! Can you imagine? Why flame holders?

Flame Holders

A perpetual revival of religion—a revival without a consequent
decline—an outpouring of the Spirit not to be withdrawn, or
relaxed, so as to bring in all of the same and of every community
and every nation, and to support all in
a steady progressive course of sanctification.[116]
Calvin Colton

The mystery of the seven stars that you saw in my right hand and
of the seven golden lampstands is this: The seven stars are the
angels of the seven churches, and the seven lampstands
are the seven churches.
Revelation 1:20

IT is not surprising that of all the word pictures Jesus
could have selected to identify the church, He chose to use
flame holders. Flame holders are free standing carriers of fire
that exist for one purpose: to hold the flame of the manifest
presence of Christ. When John turned around to see the voice
that was speaking to him—before he even locked eyes with
Christ, he saw flame holders. The last thing Jesus explained to
him after making eye contact with John was the purpose of
the flame holders.

When it is all said and done, flame holders are the essence
of what defines us as believers. Jesus not only walks among the
flame holders, He also inspects them.

If the purpose of the church was primarily to hold out propositional truth, Jesus might have walked in a library. If the church was ultimately a preaching center, He might have walked among the lecterns or the soapboxes. If the purpose of the church was primarily to deploy troops on a mission for Christ, Jesus may have walked on the deck of an aircraft carrier. If the purpose of the church was primarily to treat the wounded, He might have walked the halls of a hospital. While there are elements of truth contained in each of these word pictures, the pictures are not primary. Jesus walked among the flame holders, because the primary purpose of the church is to hold out the reality of *God on fire* so that people might encounter the manifest presence of Christ.

Luxnos

The Greek word for *flame holder* is *luxnos*, which is often misunderstood as a single-stem Jewish menorah. Bible theologian John Stott explains a luxnos, not as a "candelabra consisting of one lamp stand with seven branches (such as stood in the tabernacle outside the veil), but (as John saw) seven separate lamp stands, each no doubt with a lighted lamp, and Jesus Christ among them in the midst."[117] It would have been impossible for Christ to walk among a single-stand menorah, because He would have knocked it over. Rather, He walked among seven distinct lamp stands, or flame holders, each one representing one of the seven local churches in what is now known as Turkey to which the ,book of the Revelation was originally sent. These flame holders were freestanding pieces of furniture that held oil and were ignited to provide light to those in their vicinity. The luxnos was not the flame; it *carried* the flame. Neither was the luxnos, as Stott clarifies, a candleholder that held the object that held the flame. The luxnos itself held the flame, because the oil within it was set on fire. This is precisely the same way the local church holds the flame of God's manifest presence. The church contains the oil of the Holy Spirit, who consistently reveals Christ to us.

Because we have lost our focus as luxnos, the church today is experiencing an identity crisis. As George Barna has discovered, 23 percent of the adult population in the United States does not attend a single church activity, although nearly 60 percent of this unattached population consider themselves to be Christian.[118] This yes-to-Jesus, no-to-church movement is growing.[119] For the first time in over one hundred years, we are currently seeing a rise in the atheist movement in our country. Atheists are renting billboards, running ads and writing New York Times bestsellers. If the manifest presence of Christ is absent from the church, we can hardly blame people for being absent as well. If Jesus doesn't show up, why should we? It would be like going to Yankee Stadium to watch a baseball game in which the Yanks don't even take the field. What's the point? If God's manifest presence doesn't show up when we gather for worship, there is something seriously wrong.

This trend needs to change. There is an indivisible relationship between the local church and the manifest presence of Christ, just as there is an indivisible relationship between the luxnos and the flame. This relationship was further reinforced when Jesus warned one of the seven local churches to repent and to return to their first love of Christ, or else He would come and remove their lamp stand (see Rev. 2:5). He says the same thing today. The name of the church may still be on the marquee, and the steeple may still be on the roof, but from God's perspective, if the church fails to love and value the presence of Christ more highly than anything else, it no longer has the right to be known as a flame holder.

Jesus has irreversibly connected Himself to the church. His manifest presence is embedded in the genome of the nature of the church. One of the tragic misconceptions of revival is that it is an infrequent occurrence in the flow of church history and that encountering God's manifest presence is at times random, unpredictable or even unlikely. Such an error is as obvious as expecting a luxnos to only randomly shine. As a luxnos continually shines because it is a flame holder, the church continuously carries the flame of the manifest presence of Christ because that is who we are and what we do. A luxnos does not need to try to shine, nor does it have the ability to shine on its own. It is fully dependant on the oil and the flame.

"Flame holder" is a most vivid, defining description of the local church, one we desperately need to own. A flame holder exists for only one purpose: to hold out the blazing inferno of God's manifest presence to the community. That is it. The church will not be judged by its activity, attendance, Bible classes, technology or balance sheet. It is to carry the perpetual flame of God's manifest presence to others so that those in the neighborhoods around us look and say, "Let us go with you, because we have heard that God is with you" (Zech. 8:23).[120]

Let's get practical. The New Testament oozes with the mind-set that the church is the dwelling place of God in Christ, that His manifest presence, not just His omnipresence nor simply His indwelling presence, is what fills the church. For this reason, as we wrap up our journey into the flaming reality of *God on fire*, we should identify some vital how-to action steps your local church can implement. Once we get it—that the glorious presence of Christ wants to tangibly and conspicuously linger right in the middle of our own local church gathering—we'll always want it. We'll want it badly. Just remember, God wants it for us even more badly. We don't want to live with anything less.

The New Testament is saturated with practical, tactile instruction on how to maintain and cultivate God's tangible presence. As my graduate-school professor and mentor Richard Lovelace said, "Concentration on reformation without revival leads to skins without wine; concentration on revival without reformation soon loses the wine for want of skins."[121] So what specifically characterizes the *God on fire* environment?

God-encountering prayer and worship characterizes the God on fire *environment.* "My house will be called a house of prayer for all nations," Jesus demanded with His eyes blazing and the tendons in His neck as tight as piano wire (Mark 11:17). He then added the ominous words, "But you have made it 'a den of robbers.'" Despite most misinterpretations, a den is not where robbers go to steal but rather where they go to hide after they have stolen. Essentially Jesus was saying, "My house is to be a place to meet God, and yet you have made it a place to hide from God!"

This means that whatever activity your church is involved in, no matter how good it is in itself, if it keeps your church from becoming a house of prayer or a meeting place for God and His people, it is an idol and requires demotion. People in your church family are hiding behind that activity rather than coming face to face with the manifest presence of Christ.

Creative God-encountering worship is vital to healthy church life. It is often in the act of being worshiped that God chooses to manifest His presence to us. Church leaders always need to be asking the primary question, How can we more effectively lead our people to encounter the manifest presence of Christ in corporate worship? It is not a matter of hymns or choruses, traditional or contemporary, evangelical or Pentecostal. It goes much deeper than our labels; true worship is a matter of the heart. In my congregation in Metro Atlanta, we have a classic worship service each Sunday for our seniors so they can encounter God in life-giving, relevant ways, and we also have a contemporary worship celebration each Sunday in which others too can encounter God in life-giving, relevant ways. Even Charles Spurgeon had this desire for his church in London: "Oh for a mighty cry! A prevailing cry! A heaven-shaking cry! A cry that would make the gates of heaven open! A cry that God's arm could not resist! A cry of saints knit together in love and filled with holy passion! May theirs be the great plea of the atoning sacrifice making this the burden of their cry, 'Oh, Lord, revive Thy work in the midst of the years.'"[122]

People being filled with the Holy Spirit both corporately and individually characterizes the God on fire *environment.* When Jesus first filled His disciples with His Holy Spirit, He filled them in a corporate gathering (see Acts 2:4). When the apostle Paul exhorted the early believers to "be filled with the Spirit" (Eph. 5:18), he spoke to the church as a whole. When church means more to us than singing songs, listening to sermons and drinking coffee together, and when we shift our focus to continually encountering Christ in the middle of our gatherings, we will rediscover the joy of being continually filled with the Holy Spirit. God wants His church to restore to its proper place the work of *receiving*. Everything hinges on receiving. God has called us to extend our hands in prayer in order to heal our abilities to receive from Him. God wants to heal our receivers. Empty hands extended to Him are a visible demonstration to God that we are ready to receive a fresh revelation of Christ, to receive the Holy Spirit promptings of grace, mercy, love, power, fresh anointing and fresh faith and to receive physical healing, financial provision, ongoing repentance and much more.

John the Baptist knew this Kingdom principle when he said, "A man can receive only what is given him from heaven" (John 3:27). Jesus affirmed this Kingdom principle when he said, "Freely you have received, freely give" (Matt. 10:8). This principle has everything to do with prayer: "Ask and you will receive, and your joy will be complete" (John 16:24).

The manifestation and revelatory gifts characterize the God on fire *environment.* When you welcome the manifest presence of Christ, you throw open the door to the supernatural. Watch out! You never know exactly what may happen. The Greek word used for the nine manifestation or revelatory gifts is *phanerosis* (see 1 Cor. 12:8–10). These are the gifts that make some people nervous, because they are unknown to some. Keep in mind that they exist for one purpose: to make Christ tangibly and convincingly known. The list of gifts is most impressive:

- messages of wisdom
- healings
- distinguishing between spirits
- messages of knowledge
- miraculous powers
- tongues
- faith
- prophecy
- interpretation of tongues

When these forms of Holy Spirit manifestation are expressed properly in the local church, the Bible says that unbelievers, who will enter our fellowship like interlopers, will "fall down and worship God, exclaiming, 'God is really among you!'" (1 Cor. 14:25).

God is really among you. Now that's *church*! We all want more God-is-really-among-you moments. We get plenty of that-was-a-great-sermon, I-loved-the-music, you-have-the-best-childcare moments. We need, however, more unbelievers recognizing God is with us. Fire draws a crowd. It always has, and it always will. Some of us are so afraid of misfire or false fire that we quickly stomp out *any* fire. "Do not put out the Spirit's fire," Paul said, and he quickly added, "Do not treat prophecies with contempt" (1 Thess. 5:19–20). If we are serious about welcoming the manifest presence of Christ, we need to be prepared to welcome the manifestation gifts by which He frequently chooses to reveal Himself.

Nation-reaching characterizes the God on fire *environment.* When Jesus spoke His final pre-ascension words to His disciples, He intentionally included ever-expanding concentric circles that start in our hometown and end up around the world: "But you will receive power when the Holy Spirit comes on you; and you will be my witnesses in Jerusalem, and in all Judea and Samaria, and to the ends of the earth" (Acts 1:8).

Jerusalem was the disciples' home.
Judea was their region.
Samaria was where cross-cultural people lived in proximity to them.
The ends of the earth were all the rest of the nations.

As we have already demonstrated, the Person of the Holy Spirit is given to exalt Christ, first to us and then to others. He comes to make Jesus known in relevant, tangible ways—ways that we can get our arms around. His influence doesn't end with us. Like a nuclear bomb of righteousness, God the Holy Spirit drops on us in order to impact the nations through us. Notice the word "you" in Jesus' statement: "If I go, I will send him [the Holy Spirit] to *you*. When he comes, he will convict the world" (John 16:7–8). We often pray for the Holy Spirit to convict the world, but we miss the "*you*." God will not break protocol. The extent to which God the Holy Spirit comes and manifests Christ *in* us as believers is the extent to which God *through* us reaches the nations. We call it reaching a lost world through a revived church. Jesus calls it luxnos— flame holders. The final unreached peoples on earth will not be reached through a lukewarm church but through a revived church. My mentor, Armin Gesswein, described this process as God's Laws of Revival. Here's how it breaks down:

- The Holy Spirit brings conviction of sin to the non-Christian in the measure in which He first works in

Christians in the church.

- The unconverted feel their need for salvation when Christians first feel the need for them to be saved.
- When Christians feel a deeper need of the Holy Spirit, non-Christians will feel a need of Christ.
- When the church is first concerned for the world, then the world will be concerned for Christ.
- Non-Christian seekers will deal with their sins according to the way Christians first deal with their own.
- When Christians repent, sinners will repent.
- Sinners will pray and seek the Lord when Christians do so first.
- The unconverted will be born again of the Holy Spirit when Christians are burdened and birth them in prayer.
- When Christians are filled with the Holy Spirit, non-Christians will be convicted of sin and converted to Christ.
- When revival is strong in the church, evangelism will be strong in the world.
- When Christians walk in the light that they have, sinners will see the light in and through them.
- When God's people face the many plain Scriptures about holiness of life, cleansing from all sin, purity and victorious Christian living, sinners will face the plain Word of God regarding their salvation.
- When Christians wake up (revival), non-Christians will also wake up (evangelism).[123]

Personal

Make no mistake about it. Jesus loves flame holders. He loves community, a crowd, a party. He is not only right at home in the church, He has the unique ability to reveal Himself to every individual in the room; to speak each language, to honor each distinction, to crawl past every defense mechanism and to make Himself known to each one so that He meets every distinct, personal need.

The momentum of history is moving rapidly from the garden, where two worshipers encountered *God on fire*, to the city, where millions of worshipers will encounter *God on fire*. While God loves a party, at the same time He sends personal party invitations. If you as the reader sense God is inviting you to the *God on fire* gathering, allow me to give you a few practical action steps of your own.

Go for God's manifest presence. You were made for the manifest presence of Christ. When you get out of bed each morning, you don't need to scratch your head and wonder, *Why am I here?* You were born to know God and to encounter His manifest presence. Sing along in full-voice harmony with King David, "One thing I ask of the LORD, this is what I seek: that I may dwell in the house of the LORD all the days of my life, to gaze upon the beauty of the LORD and to seek him in his temple" (Ps. 27:4).

Be a person of one thing, not a dabbler in many things. As good as you may be at music or sales or medicine or technology or leadership or finance or education or media or law, none of these are your first calling. You are called first to wholeheartedly know God, encounter God and worship Him for who He is. If you minor in the only ultimate major, you are only kidding yourself. It is the consummate defining moment in the life of every God seeker when he or she determines to be a first-seeker. Jesus called His followers to be first-seekers. "Seek first," Jesus said, "[God's] kingdom and his righteousness, and all these things will be given to you as well" (Matt. 6:33).

All first-seekers are wholehearted seekers; there are no

other kinds. "You will seek me and find me," God declared through His flame-throwing prophet, Jeremiah, "when you seek me with all your heart" (Jer. 29:13). The reason you were born was to be an all-in first-seeker of Christ. More specifically, the reason you live in your village or city is so that at least someone in the neighborhood will declare God's glory. No matter what your career path or season in life, you have breath to praise the Lord.[124]

Be a good listener. Get your assignment straight. "He who has an ear, let him hear what the Spirit says to the churches," is what Jesus told each of the seven local churches in the book of the Revelation.[125] He told them this for good reason. Not only does God still speak, but He speaks so clearly that every believer is able to understand what He is saying. Everything hinges on us getting our assignments straight. When Jesus said about Himself, "He goes on ahead of them, and his sheep follow him because they know his voice" (John 10:4), He was affirming the all-important principle of recognizing and obeying the voice of God.

The ear is our primary receptor. The ear is the mouth of the soul, the means by which we take in spiritual food: "Listen, listen to me, and eat what is good," God says (Isa. 55:2). Even Jesus, when fasting from physical food, emphasized the importance of feeding on the Word of God, saying, "Man does not live on bread alone, but on every word that comes from the mouth of God" (Matt. 4:4).

Look for His coming. The second coming of Christ is right around the corner. The ultimate and inevitable *God on fire* moment will come when Christ physically returns. Healthy Christians long for the manifest presence of Christ. The more they see, the more they want. The more they taste, the hungrier they get. The closer they are, the more eager they become to see Him face to face in all His raging splendor and glory. Now we see but a poor reflection as in a mirror, but then we will see face to face (see 1 Cor. 13:12). The fulfillment of our growing crescendo of desire for God's presence will come when Christ returns for His second bodily visit to earth. In the meantime, each *God on fire* encounter is an approximation of the eventual return of Christ. All prayers for His manifest presence will one day be fully answered when the trumpet blows and the dead are raised and the Lord descends in a moment. A blink. A nanosecond. An instant. Every eye will see Him. For some, it will bring joy unspeakable and for others, horror.

The Greek word the Bible uses most often to refer to the return of Christ is *parousia*. I can taste it. It is used twenty-four times in the New Testament, and it literally means "presence."[126] When Christ returns, the dwelling of God will be with people (see Rev. 21:3). The kingdoms of this world will become the kingdoms of our God and of His Christ, and He shall reign forever and ever (see Rev. 11:15). Until He returns, the heart cry of God shouts out to us, "Come!" (Rev. 22:17), and the voice of the church wholeheartedly responds, "Come!" (Rev. 22:17). The Lord Jesus Christ boldly stands up and affirms, "I am coming soon" (Rev. 22:20). We resoundingly say "Maranatha! Amen! Come, Lord Jesus!" (see Rev. 22:20).

The return of Christ will be the ultimate *God on fire* moment. Until then, flame holders, let's hold the course and be true to our identity. As first-seekers, we want to encounter the manifest presence of Christ. Why settle for anything less? Like heatseeking missiles, we lock onto the heat-source. We will not be denied. For all eternity, *God on fire*, here we come!

God on Fire in History

The island of Wales experienced no less than sixteen distinct awakenings in a period of three hundred years. The most recent was in 1904–1905. The countryside of Wales was filled with groups praying nightly for revival, praying the words of Isaiah 64:1: "Rend the heavens and come down."

It was reported that "the sense of the Spirit's presence was everywhere,"[127] and yet the people hungered for more. At the age of thirteen, Evan Roberts began reading his Bible for an hour a day, praying for revival in Wales and asking God to fill him with the Holy Spirit.[128] Roberts would sing revival hymns with his friends:

> It is coming; it is coming.
> The power of the Holy Ghost.
> I receive it, I receive it.
> The power of the Holy Ghost.

At twenty-six years of age, after praying for thirteen years for the revival, the dam broke. "The room was full of the Holy Spirit. The outpouring was so powerful that I had . . . to plead with God to stay His hand."[129]

Immediately Roberts was gripped with a conviction to win souls throughout Wales. "I felt ablaze with a desire to go through the length and breadth of Wales to tell of the Savior," he said.[130] Evan Roberts led his first local church into the manifest presence of God during a Sunday evening prayer service with sixty people. He taught the people to pray the Trinitarian prayer, "O, Lord, send the Holy Spirit, now, for Christ's sake." Roberts wrote, "I felt the place being filled." People wept, sang, prayed and prostrated themselves on the floor in agony over their conviction of sin. People were converted, including notorious drunkards, prisoners, ministers, business leaders and politicians. Roberts gave people throughout Wales what became known as the *Four Articles*:[131]

1. Confess to God all unconfessed sin.
2. Give up everything doubtful.
3. Openly confess Christ.
4. Readily and immediately obey the impulse of the Holy Spirit.

Roberts challenged his best friend, Sydney Evans, "Do you believe that God can give one hundred thousand souls now?" They agreed together in prayer to see Wales won to Christ. Less than a year later, newspapers documented that in a two-month stretch, seventy thousand people were converted, eighty-five thousand in five months, and one hundred thousand in only six months.[132] The impact of God's manifest presence was deep and far reaching. Judges were given white gloves, because they went months without a single case to try. Miners complained that productivity decreased in the mines, and when they researched the reason, they discovered that it was because the miners' obscenity had been eliminated, and the mules and horses moved more slowly without the harsh treatment. [133]

Chapter Takeaways
- Flame holders are the essence of the church.
- God's manifest presence is embedded in our genome.
- "My house is to be a place to meet God, and yet you have made it a place to hide from God."
- Everything hinges on receiving.

- When you welcome the manifest presence of Christ, you throw open the door to the supernatural.
- All first-seekers are wholehearted seekers; there are no other kinds.
- The ultimate *God on fire* moment will come when Christ physically returns.
- The hope of the world is the manifest presence of Christ in the middle of the church.

* * * * *

As I wrapped up the research for this book, I found myself sitting in a scary place: the basement library of Gordon-Conwell Theological Seminary. This was the exact place where thirty-five years earlier I had read tens of thousands of pages including *The Complete Works of Jonathan Edwards, City of God* by Augustine and hundreds of other books. I wrote dozens of papers till I was bleary-eyed. I crammed for innumerable Greek and Hebrew exams and took more than my share of naps.

Three years of great memories flooded over me as I sat.

I suddenly remembered that this place was where I had first discovered the revival history of Count Nicholas Ludwig von Zinzendorf, Saint Patrick, Wesley, Whitefield and the others. It was where I had discovered that what drove these men was the manifest presence of Christ. As I sat there, I thought of all the dreams for the local church I'd had as a young seminarian—dreams of growth, health, accelerated change, city transformation and revival. I thought of the all-nighters fueled by endless cups of coffee and the heated cafeteria discussions on the fine points of theology. The most vivid memories were of the moments in which I had encountered God right there at the seminary, often in the library.

This room was a scary place because I was surrounded by fifty thousand books about Christ and His church, many of them pointing to *God on fire*, and I found myself wondering how many students would come and go and never actually encounter Him.

It was scary because 98 percent of those books had been sitting there thirty-five years ago when I had been an idealistic student preparing to go into the world to make a difference.

It was scary because there were (and are) hundreds of churches throughout New England within the shadow of the seminary who had yet to encounter the flaming reality of God's presence. Many had closed their doors, and many of their pastors had dropped out of the ministry.

After thirty-five years of pastoral ministry and after serving local churches in forty countries of the world through the College of Prayer, I could see more clearly than ever that the manifest presence of Christ was far more than a pipe dream of a zealous graduate student. It was and is the power cell of the church. The hope of the world is the church of Jesus Christ and, more specifically, the manifest presence of Christ in the middle of the church. The future of the church rests with its leaders who will receive the flame, value it and share it with the nations. We are incurably flame holders, and our relevance is determined entirely by our disposition to flame.

If you dare, use this one hundred fifty year-old prayer by Charles Spurgeon as your own:

> *O God, send us the Holy Spirit! Give us both the breath of spiritual life and the fire of unconquerable zeal. You are our God. Answer us by fire, we pray to you! Answer us both by wind and fire, and then we will see you to be God indeed. The Kingdom comes not, and the work is flagging. Oh, that you would send the wind and the fire! And you will do this when we are all of one accord, all believing, all expecting, all prepared by prayer.[134]*

Epilogue

It is one thing for Moses and Aaron, Elijah and Abraham, David and Solomon, Isaiah and Malachi or even the apostle John to meet *God on fire*, but that was then and this is now. Were their experiences isolated incidents, aberrations or exceptions? How do we know that encountering God's manifest presence is intended for the rest of us?

Glad you asked.

It's important that we have a reasonable, biblical understanding of the fact that God's manifest presence is intended to be the normal Christian experience. In order to acquire this understanding, one must consider the nature of God and the nature of humanity by investigating both the beginning of the human species and its end. We will visit a garden and a city. The garden is where humanity first began; the city is where it will end. Like bookends that surround all the volumes and annals of recorded human history, these markers on either end of the expanse of time will give us our perspective. Since the Bible gives a detailed account of both ends of the timeline of humanity, it will be enlightening for us to explore what the record shows. I'm certain we will discover that both the garden and the city have much in common, one being that they are both venues in which people encounter God in all His glory.

The Garden

Humanity started in a garden. Many people enjoy playing in the dirt, but for God there was more at stake than tomatoes and bell peppers. God wanted relationship. More specifically, He wanted worship. Having already created the field mouse and the pelican, God said, "Let us make man in our image, in our likeness" (Gen. 1:26). He scooped dirt into His hands, fashioned it into a human body, put His lips over man's nostrils and exhaled. Man instantly became a living being. God created them male and female, calling them Adam and Eve. God was immediately pleased with what He had made, and He saw that "it was very good" (Gen. 1:31).

God gave Adam and Eve the ability to hear more than the chirp of the chickadee and the roar of the lion; He gave them the unique ability to hear the voice of God. He said, "Be fruitful and increase in number; fill the earth and subdue it. Rule over the fish of the sea and the birds of the air and over every living creature that moves on the ground" (Gen. 1:28). Having given them responsibility, He also gave them limitations: "And the LORD God commanded the man, 'You are free to eat from any tree in the garden; but you must not eat from the tree of the knowledge of good and evil, for when you eat of it you will surely die'" (Gen. 2:16–17).

Unlike some wealthy estate owners who put caretakers in charge and never revisit their property, God frequently visited the garden. Adam and Eve became so familiar with the manifest presence of God that even after their disobedience, they were still capable of recognizing God's tangible presence with them in the garden. The account reads, "Then the man and his wife heard the sound of the LORD God as he [God] was walking in the garden in the cool of the day" (Gen. 3:8). The garden was a temple-garden in which God revealed His presence to the man and the woman. In response the man and woman worshiped, obeyed and trusted God.

In this account of the origins of the human species, we discover that there is something embedded deep in our DNA that separates us from the warthog and the cocker spaniel.

We were given the ability to hear God and we were given the discernment to recognize precisely what He is saying. This account in Genesis dramatically illustrates that we were created with the distinct ability to recognize God's presence—His tangible, specific, local, personal, manifest presence. The worship of God by Adam and Eve was entirely predicated on their ability to know the reality of God's manifest presence.

Just pause for a moment. Imagine yourself walking with God in a garden in the cool of the day. Not only does this prototype garden teach us about our own DNA, it instructs us as well on the nature of God.

God has a purpose. Nothing is by accident—including you. God's purpose from the beginning was to create an environment in which He could reveal His presence to His people. The lettuce and green beans in the garden were only part of His plan. His fuller purpose was to manifest His presence to His people and to provide a venue in which they could enjoy that ongoing relationship. The self-revealing God demonstrated from the very beginning of creation that He intended to draw people into consistent, vital relationship with Himself by explicitly manifesting to them His glorious presence.

The City

Let's zoom ahead at least ten thousand years. Humanity began in a garden, but it will end in a city. The opening chapters of the first book in the Bible, the book of Genesis, describe the garden. The closing chapters of the last book in the Bible, the book of the Revelation, describe the city.

This city is unlike any other. There are no crime, no traffic jams and no pollution. There are no police, no fire-and-rescue squads and no gangs. Instead of asphalt and potholes, the streets are paved with solid gold. Instead of gutters full of cigarette butts and gum wrappers, there is a river as clear as crystal. Instead of weeds growing on an expressway divider, there is a lush green tree which bears fruit year round and whose leaves are for the healing of the nations. As good and enticing as all this sounds, there is one benefit that will eclipse all the others: the manifest presence of God will fill the place. John writes, "And I heard a loud voice from the throne saying, 'Now the dwelling of God is with men, and he will live with them. They will be his people, and God himself will be with them and be their God'" (Rev. 21:3). This describes the ultimate never-ending encounter with God's manifest presence. "The kingdom of the world has become the kingdom of our Lord and of his Christ, and he will reign for ever and ever" (Rev. 11:15).

The account goes on to describe in vivid detail the particulars of this magnificent mega-city:

> *I did not see a temple in the city, because the Lord God Almighty and the Lamb are its temple. The city does not need the sun or the moon to shine on it, for the glory of God gives it light, and the Lamb is its lamp. The nations will walk by its light, and the kings of the earth will bring their splendor into it. On no day will its gates ever be shut, for there will be no night there. (Rev. 21:22–25)*

This is a lot to wrap our minds around. Several pieces of the puzzle may be surprising, even confusing.

No temple? No church, no mosque and no synagogue? Exactly. A place of worship is a localized place to meet with God. On that day, however, when the dwelling of God is with men, God's manifest presence will no longer be localized. We won't ever again need to go to church; we will be the church. The manifest presence of God will be as plentiful on that day as the omnipresence of God is today.

No sun or moon? No streetlights, no headlights and no

night-lights? Exactly. Light exists now because darkness exists. On that day, however, when the light of the knowledge of the glory of the Lord shines in the face of Jesus Christ for all to see, there will no longer be any darkness. There will be no atheists, no hypocrites, no fakers nor idolaters. We will never again need to turn on a light, replace a light bulb or pay an electric bill. We will be living in the Light, the light of God's presence. Always.

The megacity, the eternal city, is a place where God will manifest His presence. Just as God planted a temple-garden on the front end of human history, so the city God will establish on the back end of human history will be a temple-city. When the gun went off at the start of the human race, and when it goes off again at the finish line, the same truth will remain: humanity was made for the manifest presence of God. God's manifest presence is there at the beginning and at the end.

As we consider this finale of human history, let's consider the words of that great "philosopher", Yogi Berra, "It's déjà vu all over again!" We will soon return to our roots. We, who were originally at home in God's manifest presence in the temple-garden, will be at home in God's manifest presence in the temple-city. The entire story of human history, moving from one venue to the other, is being written by a personal, self-revealing God who invites each of us into His story.

First and Last

When the apostle John first laid eyes on the exalted Christ, he was paralyzed with fear. Awestruck. To reorient John and to let him know that he had not lost his mind or his view of reality, Jesus said, "Do not be afraid" (Rev. 1:17). He assured John that he had, in fact, encountered a higher reality. Then Jesus added the self-revealing words, "I am the First and the Last" (Rev. 1:17). Like bookends that hold together all the annals of human history, Jesus is the First who revealed Himself in the temple-garden, and He is the Last who will reveal Himself in the temple-city.

"I am the First," Jesus said. That is to say, "I always go first. I am the chief apostle. I am the initiator. I created the worlds and all that is in them. In the middle of My original creation, I planted a garden, the temple-garden where I walked with My people in the cool of the day. I manifested My presence to them and spoke with them in words they could understand. I am the First. I want you to understand the perspective of your life now in the light of where the human race began."

"I am the Last," Jesus said. That is to say, "I leave nothing unfinished. I will see through to completion everything I start. My will and My purposes will be done. There is coming a day when the dwelling of God will be with people. They will be My people. I will be with them, and I will be their God. My manifest presence will forever dwell with them without end. I am the Last. I want you to live now in the light of the reality of where the human race will end."

We have great cause for sober reflection as we gaze upon our beginning and upon our end via the lens of God's Word. One day history as we know it will come to an end. Armies will put down their weapons for the last time. Every hospital will close its doors. Every prison will open its doors. Civilization will encounter something it has not witnessed since the garden. The knowledge of the glory of the Lord will cover the earth as the waters cover the sea (see Hab. 2:14). God will remove the cataracts from our eyes, and we will see Jesus the way John did on the island. The headline in every newspaper in every city in every language in every nation will be the same: "God Is with Us." Ready or not, this is our future.

Final Takeaways

- The manifest presence of Christ is the normal Christian experience.
- The original garden was a temple garden.
- The final city is a temple city.
- Like bookends around the flow of human history, we discover that God's manifest presence is in our DNA for time and eternity.

Appendix A

Significant Encounters with God's Manifest Presence in the Old Testament

Adam and Eve, Genesis 2–3
Enoch, Genesis 5:21–24
Noah, Genesis 6:8–9
Abraham, Genesis 12–22
Jacob, Genesis 28–32
Moses, Exodus 3
Israel at Sinai, Exodus 32–34
Samuel, 1 Samuel 3
Elijah, 1 Kings 18
King Josiah, 2 Kings 22
The temple dedication, 2 Chronicles 5–7
King Asa, 2 Chronicles 15
Zerubbabel, Ezra 3
Ezra, Ezra 9–10
Nehemiah, the book of Nehemiah
The prophet Isaiah, Isaiah 6
The prophet Ezekiel, Ezekiel 1
Ninevah, the book of Jonah

Appendix B

Significant Encounters with God's Manifest Presence in the New Testament

John the Baptist, Matthew 3; Mark 1:1–8; Luke 3:1–20;
John 1:15–36; 3:22–36

The Lord Jesus Christ, the four Gospels

Upper-room Christians at Pentecost, Acts 1–2

Philip, the Samaritan revival and the Ethiopian eunuch, Acts
8

Saul becomes Paul, Acts 9:1-31

Cornelius's house, Acts 10

Antioch, Acts 13

Philippi, Acts 16:8-40

Thessalonica, Acts 17:1-9

Corinth, Acts 18:1-17

Ephesus, Acts 18:18–19

John on Patmos, Revelation 1

Appendix C

The Manifest Presence Manifesto
February 7–10, 2012

In the name of God the Father, God the Son and God the Holy Spirit, we declare and confess that it is the sovereign purpose of God that the glory of His manifest presence fill the earth (Hab. 2:14). Because prayer is the highest priority to accomplish this, the risen Lord Jesus Christ gave the mandate in Acts 1:4 not to leave Jerusalem but to wait for the promise of the Father. In obedience to this mandate, the disciples gathered together and prayed in what would become known as the Upper Room. While they were praying, God poured out His Holy Spirit; and out from there, He sent forth His empowered church. It is in the upper room that we ask for the nations (Ps. 2:8]).

We are called by the Lord Jesus Christ to make Upper Room disciples among the nations so that the Church experiences genuine revival and becomes a house of prayer for all nations. We seek the presence of God, not titles or positions. We prefer action to mere words, compassionate service instead of control and effective prayer rather than religiosity. We assume responsibility rather than placing blame, and we want to invest what we have rather than to seek handouts.

Our vision is clear—to mentor, train and equip Christian pastors and leaders to reach a lost world through a revived church.

Our assignment is compelling—to build God-encountering Upper Room disciples and to build Upper

Room prayer environments among the nations.

Our strategy is specific—to plant campuses of the College of Prayer in every nation as the Lord opens doors.

We have not chosen this assignment for ourselves; Christ has entrusted this to us. He has appointed and anointed us, therefore we wholeheartedly give ourselves to fulfill this assignment with all the energy Christ supplies to us.

The revival we are working toward is not superficial, short lived or limited to one place or people group. This revival will be pride breaking, sin removing, Satan evicting, stronghold overthrowing, life transforming, leader developing, church awakening and nation discipling. We realize this call is worth any sacrifice, and we resolve in advance to pay the price required; and by the grace of God we will persevere until the job is done.

We earnestly desire this revival of God's manifest presence in our generation, and we give ourselves fully to see this vision fulfilled.

This document was originally crafted at the Leadership Summit of the College of Prayer International, February 7–10, 2012 in Atlanta, Georgia, USA. It is available online for you to sign at www.CollegeofPrayer.org.

Appendix D

Study Guide Questions

Rather than include study guide questions in this book, they are available online at www.CollegeofPrayer.org. Many other free and useful prayer-mobilizing tools are also available.

Endnotes

1. Stephen and Andrew were both students at Wheaton College when this project began. Though they have since graduated, they and their generation were the faces I saw as I wrote every page. Their inspiration motivated the writing of this book, and they deserve the dedication.

Introduction

2. David Bryant, *Hope at Hand* (Grand Rapids: Baker, 1995), 31.
3. Ibid., 31.
4. Ibid., 31.
5. Ibid., 31.
6. This took place on a runway of the International Airport in Seoul, Korea. My dear friend and the lead elder in my church, Dale Webb, and his wife, Beverly, were present for this historic prayer gathering.

Chapter One

7. Richard Owen Roberts, *Repentance* (Wheaton, IL: Crossway, 2002), 17.
8. A.W. Tozer, *The Pursuit of God* (Camp Hill, PA: Christian Publications, 1982), 60.
9. R.J. Krejcir, Ph.D., "Statistics on Pastors," Francis A. Schaeffer Institute of Church Leadership Development http://www.churchleadership.org/apps/articles/default.asp?articleid=42347&..=&contentonly=true, (research from 1989 to 2006).
10. This statistic was told to me by three different sources and matches my own research in working with thousands of pastors from all over the world.
11. George Barna, "Twentysomethings Struggle to Find Their Place in Christian Churches," http://www.barna.org/barna-update/article/5-barna-update/127-twentysomethings-struggle-to-find-their-place-in-christian-churches.
12. Bill Hybels, *Courageous Leadership* (Grand Rapids: Zondervan, 2002), 27.
13. Tozer, *The Pursuit of God*, 61.

14. Henry T. Blackaby and Claude B. King, *Experiencing God: Knowing and Doing the Will of God* (Nashville: LifeWay, 1990), 78.

15. Jonathan Edwards, *The Works of Jonathan Edwards, Vol. 2* (Edinburgh: Banner of Truth, 1976), 283.

16. Richard F. Lovelace, *Dynamics of Spiritual Life* (Downers Grove, IL: Intervarsity Press, 1979), 35–39.

17. Ibid., 35–39.

18. Richard Owen Roberts, *Glory Filled the Land* (Wheaton, IL: International Awakening Press, 1989).

19. Eifion Evans, *Revival Comes to Wales* (Bridgend: Evangelical Press of Wales, 1982), 70.

20. Roberts, *Glory Filled the Land*.

21. J. Edwin Orr, *Evangelical Awakening in India* (New Delhi: Masihi Sahitya Sanstha Christian Literature Institute, 1970), 89.

22. Douglas J. Nelson, "The Story of Bishop William J. Seymour of the Azusa Street Revival: A Search for Pentecostal/Charismatic Roots," A Doctoral Dissertation of Philosophy in the Faculty of Arts Department of Theology, University of Birmingham, England, May 1981, 271n124.

23. Christmas Evans in *Heartcry: A Journal on Revival and Spiritual Awakening* (Fall 2007).

24. Lovelace, *Dynamics of Spiritual Life*, 35–39.

25. *Christian History Magazine* 1, no. 1 (1984): 3–4.

26. Andrew Murray, *Key to the Missionary Problem* (Fort Washington, PA: Christian Literature Crusade, 1979), 49–69.

27. Ibid., 43–86.

28. John R. Weinlick, *Count Zinzendorf: The Story of His Life and Leadership in the Renewed Moravian Church* (Bethlehem, PA: The Moravian Church in America, 1984); A.J. Lewis, *Zinzendorf, The Ecumenical Pioneer* (Philadelphia: Westminster Press, 1962). Nicholas Ludwig Von Zinzendorf was part of a movement known as German Pietism. He was taught and discipled at Halle University by August H. Francke, a Lutheran clergyman and Bible scholar, who taught small group Bible study, national-impact prayer meetings and itinerant evangelism. At nine years old, Francke was so in love with Jesus he asked his mother for a room that he could use exclusively for prayer.
    Francke was mentored by Philipp Spener who in 1675 wrote the influential revival manifesto *Pia Desideria* (or *Pious Desires*) emphasizing the need for repentance, holiness, Biblical education,

missional advancement and social concern in the context of a vital impartation of the manifest presence of God. Historians have called this work "a Lutheran bolt of lightning."

The contributions of Pietism are far-reaching and include the seven core values of small group discipleship, prayer groups with a world evangelism focus, short-term mission teams, Christian hymnology, social action, world missions, and scripture distribution. This stream of German Pietism flowed parallel to that of English Puritanism with its own team of equally impactful leaders such as Laurence Humphry (1527-1590), president of Magdalen College in Oxford; Thomas Cartwright (1535-1603), Professor of Theology in Cambridge; Tom Wilcox (1549-1608), a London pastor; William Travers (1548-1635), a Cambridge professor; and John Bunyan (1628-88), a writer and preacher known for his book, *Pilgrims Progress.* Each of these champions lifted up their voices like a trumpet to call people to a fresh encounter with Christ.

Chapter Two

29. A. Douglas Brown, *Revival Addresses* (London: Morgan and Scott, 1922), 8.

30. McDowell and Reid, *FireFall*, 104.

31. James O'Leary, *The Most Ancient Life of St. Patrick* (New York: P.J. Kennedy, 1881), 135.

32. Alexander Roberts and James Donaldson, *Ante-Nicene Fathers*, vol. 1 (Buffalo: Christian Literature Publishing Company, 1885, 1896), 310, 213, 4.

33. Ibid., 313.

34. McDowell and Reid, *FireFall*, 98, 99.

Chapter Three

35. C.S. Lewis, *Letters to Malcolm, Chiefly on Prayer* (Orlando: Harcourt, 1963), 82.

36. Charles Finney, *Charles G. Finney: An Autobiography* (Old Tappan, NJ: Fleming H. Revell Co., 1908), 20.

37. Charles G. Finney, *Revival Fire* (Waukesha, WI: Metropolitan Church Association, n.d.), 10–11.

38. Lovelace, *Dynamics of Spiritual Life*, 82.

39. Elisabeth Elliot, *Through Gates of Splendor* (Grand Rapids: Zondervan, 1958), 58–59.

40.   R.A. Torrey, "Why God Used D.L. Moody," http://www.
      wholesomewords.org/biography/biomoody6.html.

41.   V. Raymond Edman, *They Found the Secret* (Grand Rapids:
      Zondervan, 1984), 101.

42.   Ibid., 104.

43.   Torrey, "Why God Used D.L. Moody."

Chapter Four

44.   Leanne Payne, *The Healing Presence* (Grand Rapids: Baker, 1989),
      53.

45.   *Christian History Magazine* 4 (November 3, 1985).

46.   A.W. Tozer, *Experiencing the Presence of God* (Ventura, CA: Regal,
      2010), 9.

47.   Malcolm McDowell and Alvin Reid, *Firefall* (Nashville: Broadman
      & Holman, 1997), 256.

48.   Ibid., 251.

49.   Ibid., 261.

50.   Talbot W. Chambers, *The Noon Prayer Meeting of the North Dutch
      Reformed Church* (New York: Border Publications of the Reformed
      Protestant Dutch Church, 1958), 196–197.

Chapter Five

51.   John Telford, *The Life of John Wesley* (London: Epworth Press,
      1886), 117.

52.   N.H. Keeble, Ed., *The Autobiography of Richard Baxter* (London:
      Dent Publishers, 1974), 79.

53.   Edwards, *The Works of Jonathan Edwards, Vol. 1* (Edinburgh: Banner
      of Truth, 1976), 370.

54.   *The Englishman's Hebrew and Chaldee Concordance of the Old
      Testament* (Grand Rapids: Zondervan, 1970).

55.   Library of Christian Classics, vol. 6, 248.

56.   J.H.S. Burleigh, Ed., *Augustine: Earlier Writings* (Philadelphia:
      Westminster Press, 1953) 55.

57.   Ibid, 431–450.

58.   Ibid, 450

Chapter Six

59.   Edman, *They Found the Secret*, 52.

60. See Acts 2:33; 7:55; Colossians 3:1; Hebrews 10:12; 1 Peter 3:22.

61. Henri J.M. Nouwen, *In the Name of Jesus* (New York: Crossroad, 1998).

62. Clark Williams, *The Descent of the Dove: A Short History of the Holy Spirit in the Church* (Grand Rapids: Eerdmans, 1968), 217.

63. See 1 Corinthians 6:20.

64. All seventy resolutions are recorded word for word in the extensive memoirs of Jonathan Edwards in *The Works of Jonathan Edwards*, xi–cccxxxiii.

65. Brian H. Edwards, *Revival! A People Saturated with God* (Carlisle, PA: Evangelical Press, 1990) 54.

66. Edwards, *The Works of Jonathan Edwards*, Vol. 2, 283.

67. Ibid., 576.

68. Ibid., 282.

69. Ibid., 283.

70. Edwards, *The Works of Jonathan Edwards*, Vol. 1, 348.

71. Ibid., 364.

72. Edwards, *The Works of Jonathan Edwards*, Vol. 1, 370.

Chapter Seven

73. Spoken at a conference for missionaries in New York as quoted in Murray, *The Key to the Missionary Problem*, 88.

74. Oswald Chambers, *My Utmost for His Highest* (New York: Dodd and Meade, 1935).

75. Leanne Payne, *Listening Prayer* (Grand Rapids: Baker, 1994), 209.

76. Ibid., 211.

77. Ibid., 52–53.

78. This F.B. Meyer quote is found in several sources, including a message by Billy Graham, but the primary source has never been documented to the author's knowledge.

79. Charles Spurgeon, *The Power of Prayer in the Believer's Life* (Lynnwood, WA: Emerald Books, 1993), 195.

80. Remember that the word baptize was a very common commercial word in the first century. Ships that were sunk at sea were baptized, or immersed. Clothing that was dyed a color was baptized, or saturated in the dye. Unfortunately, we have made the word so religious that we are in danger of missing the point. God wants us to be immersed, saturated, baptized, filled to beyond the saturation point with His Holy Spirit.

81. *The Works of Jonathan Edwards*, lxiii.

82. Ibid., lxv.

Chapter Eight

83. Blackaby, *Experiencing God*.
84. "History of Facebook," http://en.wikipedia.org/wiki/History_of_Facebook (accessed April 2012).
85. Edman, *They Found the Secret*, 52.
86. Murray, *The Key to the Missionary Problem*, 19.
87. Nehemiah Kurnock, ed., *The Journal of John Wesley*, vol. 1 (London: The Epworth Press, 1938), 475–476.
88. McDowell and Reid, *Firefall*, 198.

Chapter Nine

89. Smith Wigglesworth, *Smith Wigglesworth Devotional* (New Kensington, PA: Whitaker, 1999), 437.
90. Heard twenty years ago at a life-giving "Basic Life Principles" Seminar with Bill Gothard.
91. I was part of the Pastors' Prayer Summit that became part of the International Renewal Ministries, which has been catalytic in developing God-encountering prayer gatherings all over the world.
92. Wesley Duewel, Revival Fire (Grand Rapids, MI: Zondervan, 1995), 65
93. Benjamin Franklin, The Works of Franklin (Chicago: Townsend, 1882), 138.
94. Duewel, *Revival Fire*, 64

Chapter Ten

95. Michael L. Brown, *From Holy Laughter to Holy Fire* (Shippensburg, PA: Destiny Image, 1996), 168.
96. "The Ritz-Carlton Hotel Company, L.L.C. History," http://www.fundinguniverse.com/company-histories/The-RitzCarlton-Hotel-Company-LLC-Company-History.html.
97. Ibid.
98. "When the Spirit Fell," *Pentecostal Evangelism* (April 6, 1946): 6.
99. Douglas J. Nelson, "The Story of Bishop William J. Seymour of the Azusa Street Revival: A Search for Pentecostal/Charismatic Roots," A Doctoral Dissertation of Philosophy in the Faculty of Arts Department of Theology, University of Birmingham, England, May 1981, 192–196.

100. Ibid., 57.
101. Ibid., 209n116.
102. Ibid., 197n88.
103. Ibid., 1–50.

Chapter Eleven

104. St. Augustine of Hippo, *The City of God* (New York: Modern Library, 1950).
105. Jesus again uses the word picture of keys and doors in Revelation 3:7–8. The open door refers to doors of missional opportunity.
106. Murray, *The Key to the Missionary Problem*, 18.
107. Ibid., 77–78.
108. Ibid., 21.
109. Ibid., 111.
110. David Bryant, *Concerts of Prayer* (Ventura, CA: Regal, 1984).
111. *The Works of Jonathan Edwards Volume 2* (Edinburgh: Banner of Truth, 1976), 278.
112. See Matthew 16:17. We further learn how frail Peter's natural intelligence and human ingenuity were when he rebuked Christ for the thought of going to the cross, to which Jesus replied, "Get behind me, Satan." Within a single conversation, Peter heard from God and expressed truth, and a moment later heard from Satan and expressed error.
113. McDowell and Reid, *FireFall*, 120.
114. Ibid, 119.
115. Eric Doyle, *St. Francis and the Song of Brotherhood* (New York: The Seabury Press, 1981), 26–27.

Chapter Twelve

116. Calvin Colton, *History and Character of American Revivals of Religion*, 2nd ed. (London: Frederick Westley and A.H. Davis, 1838), 141–143.
117. John R.W. Stott, *What Christ Thinks of the Church* (Downers Grove, IL: InterVarsity, 1958), 18.
118. http://www.barna.org/congregations-articles/45-new-statistics-on-church-attendance-and-avoidance?q=church+attendance
119. Sadly, four out of ten unchurched people report that they are no longer involved in a church because of a hurtful or unpleasant experience that occurred while they were attending a church.

120. This was the primary, visionary, faith-building Bible verse that Jonathan Edwards claimed during the season known as America's First Great Awakening.

121. Lovelace, *Dynamics of Spiritual Life*, 16.

122. Charles Spurgeon, *The Power of Prayer in the Believer's Life* (Lynnwood, WA: Emerald Books, 1993), 89. Charles Haddon Spurgeon was a most remarkable preacher, selling twenty-five thousand copies of his printed sermons every week, which were translated into more than twenty languages. His congregation numbered six thousand and more, gaining well over fourteen thousand members during his thirty-eight-year ministry in London. Over 3,561 sermons of his were recorded in sixty-three volumes. In Spurgeon's lifetime he preached to an estimated 10 million people and remains history's most widely read preacher.

123. Fred Hartley, *Everything by Prayer* (Lilburn, GA: Revival Prayer Institute, 2003), 27–28.

124. See Psalm 150.

125. See Revelation 2:7, 11, 17, 29; 3:6, 13, 22.

126. William F. Arndt and F. Wilbur Gingrich, *A Greek-English Lexicon of the New Testament* (Chicago: University of Chicago Press, 1957).

127. Wesley Duewel, *Revival Fire* (Grand Rapids: Zondervan, 1995), 183–184.

128. Ibid., 185.

129. Evans, *Revival Comes to Wales*, 70.

130. Duewel, *Revival Fire*, 186.

131. Robert, *Glory Filled the Land*, 44.

132. McDowell and Reid, *FireFall*, 278.

133. Arthur Goodrich, *The Story of the Welsh Revival* (New York: Fleming H. Revell Company, 1905), 46.

134. David Bryant, *The Hope at Hand* (Grand Rapids: Baker, 1995), 182–184.

This book was produced by CLC Publications. We hope it has been life-changing and has given you a fresh experience of God through the work of the Holy Spirit. CLC Publications is an outreach of CLC Ministries International, a global literature mission with work in over fifty countries. If you would like to know more about us or are interested in opportunities to serve with a faith mission, we invite you to contact us at:

CLC Ministries International
PO Box 1449
Fort Washington, PA 19034

———

Phone: 215-542-1242
E-mail: orders@clcpublications.com
Website: www.clcpublications.com

- - - - - - - - - - - - - - - - - -

DO YOU LOVE GOOD CHRISTIAN BOOKS?
Do you have a heart for worldwide missions?

You can receive a FREE subscription to
CLC's newsletter on global literature missions
Order by e-mail at:

clcworld@clcusa.org
Or fill in the coupon below and mail to:

**PO Box 1449
Fort Washington, PA 19034**

┌─ ─ ─ ─ ─ ─ ─ ─ ─ ─ ─ ─ ─ ─ ─ ─ ─┐

FREE *CLC WORLD* SUBSCRIPTION!

Name: _____

Address:_____

_____

Phone: _____ **E-mail:**_____

└─ ─ ─ ─ ─ ─ ─ ─ ─ ─ ─ ─ ─ ─ ─ ─ ─┘

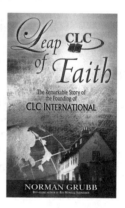